D0721909

R. Henry Migliore, PhD
Robert E. Stevens, PhD
David L. Loudon, PhD

Church and Ministry Strategic Planning: From Concept to Success

More pre-publication
REVIEWS, COMMENTARIES, EVALUATIONS . . .

"**P**uts a powerful tool in the hands of churches and pastors. Takes the technical jargon of strategic planning and makes the basic concepts accessible to the non-professional. PROVIDES THE TOOLS FOR APPLYING THE MATERIAL TO THE LOCAL CHURCH OR RELIGIOUS MINISTRY CONTEXT."

Wade R. Paschal, Jr., PhD
Senior Pastor,
First United Methodist Church,
Ardmore, Oklahoma

"**F**or people who are eager to learn how to be more effective in their ministry. It challenged me to set the right kind of goals. I especially thought the chapter on establishing objectives was excellent. I RECOMMEND IT TO EVERYONE WHO WANTS TO BE MORE THAN ONE STEP AHEAD OF THE CROWD."

Eric A. Capaci, MD
Pastor,
Gospel Light Baptist Church,
Hot Springs, Arkansas

"**D**esigned to minimize your time investment with easy-to-undersand "how to do it" steps and a multitude of relevant examples. Implementing strategic planning, as shown by the authors will, with God's help, ENABLE YOUR LEADERSHIP TEAM TO BE THE CATALYST TO MOVE YOUR ORGANIZATION INTO THE 21st CENTURY AND MAKE A DIFFERENCE IN YOUR SPHERE OF INFLUENCE."

Carle M. Hunt, DBA
Professor,
College of Administration
and Management,
Regent University

More pre-publication
REVIEWS, COMMENTARIES, EVALUATIONS . . .

"**C**HURCH AND MINISTRY STRA-
TEGIC PLANNING SEPARATES
THE WHEAT FROM THE CHAFF WITH
REGARD TO STRATEGIC PLANNING.
Migliore, Stevens, and Loudon explain
and illustrate the strategic planning
process (defining purpose, analyzing
and clarifying assumptions, establishing
objectives, formulating strategy, and
appraising and controlling) in concise,
clear, and convincing language.

Ministers need not wince at im-
porting "secular management tools"
into their ministries, for [this book]
links Scripture and planning principles in convincing ways. The authors also achieve their objective to
present material that is both theoretically sound and practically oriented.
The strategic plans of actual churches
included in the text alone make the
book worth its price."

Leslie A. Andrews
Vice Provost and Director,
Doctor of Ministry Program,
Asbury Theological Seminary,
Wilmore, Kentucky

"**T**HIS BOOK IS INDICATIVE
OF THE AUTHORS' VAST
EXPERIENCE AS CONSULTANTS
AND THEIR DESIRE TO PRO-
VIDE HELPFUL ASSISTANCE TO
CHURCHES AND MINISTRIES.
The distinction they make between
strategic decisions and tactical decisions is an example of the in-
sights they offer. It is easy for
churches and ministries to become
so action oriented that they do not
relate their activities to a strategy
that emanates from organizational
purpose. Theoretical constructs,
models, and forms provide sufficient resources to guide a leadership team through the productive
process of strategic planning."

Charles W. Snow, EdD
Dean of Doctoral Studies,
School of Theology and Missions,
Oral Roberts University

The Haworth Press, Inc.

Church and Ministry Strategic Planning
From Concept to Success

HAWORTH Marketing and Resources
Innovations in Practice & Professional Services

William J. Winston, Senior Editor

New, Recent, and Forthcoming Titles:

Long Term Care Administration: The Management of Institutional and Non-Institutional Components of the Continuum of Care by Ben Abramovice

Cases and Select Readings in Health Care Marketing, edited by Robert E. Sweeney, Robert L. Berl, and William J. Winston

Marketing Planning Guide by Robert E. Stevens, David L. Loudon, and William E. Warren

Marketing for Churches and Ministries by Robert E. Stevens and David L. Loudon

The Clinician's Guide to Managed Mental Health Care by Norman Winegar

A Guide to Preparing Cost-Effective Press Releases by Robert H. Loeffler

How to Create Interest-Evoking, Sales-Inducing, Non-Irritating Advertising by Walter Weir

Professional Services Marketing: Strategy and Tactics by F. G. Crane

Market Analysis: Assessing Your Business Opportunities by Robert E. Stevens, Philip K. Sherwood, and J. Paul Dunn

Framework for Market-Based Hospital Pricing Decisions by Shahram Heshmat

Marketing for Attorneys and Law Firms, edited by William J. Winston

Selling Without Confrontation by Jack Greening

Persuasive Advertising for Entrepreneurs and Small Business Owners: How to Create More Effective Sales Messages by Jay P. Granat

Marketing Mental Health Services in a Managed Care Environment by Norman Winegar and John L. Bistline

Church and Ministry Strategic Planning: From Concept to Success by R. Henry Migliore, Robert E. Stevens, and David L. Loudon

Church and Ministry Strategic Planning
From Concept to Success

R. Henry Migliore, PhD
Robert E. Stevens, PhD
David L. Loudon, PhD

The Haworth Press
New York • London • Norwood (Australia)

The Haworth Press, Inc., 10 Alice Street, Binghamton, NY 13904-1580

Library of Congress Cataloging-in-Publication Data

Migliore, R. Henry.
    Church and ministry strategic planning : from concept to success / R. Henry Migliore, Robert E. Stevens, David L. Loudon.
       p.   cm.
    Includes bibliographical references and index.
    ISBN 1-56024-346-5 (alk. paper)
    1. Church management. 2. Strategic planning. I. Stevens, Robert E., 1942- . II. Loudon, David L. III. Title.
BV652.M53 1994
254–dc20
                                                     93-17360
                                                        CIP

CONTENTS

ABOUT THE AUTHORS

R. Henry Migliore, PhD, is Professor of Strategic Planning and Management at Northeastern State University/University Center at Tulsa where he teaches both graduate and undergraduate courses. He was formerly Dean of the Oral Roberts University (ORU) School of Business and a Visiting Professor at the University of Calgary. He is the author of numerous articles and books on management of both profit and nonprofit organizations, and has worked with many churches and ministries in developing strategic plans.

Robert E. Stevens, PhD, is Professor of Marketing in the College of Business Administration at Northeast Louisiana University in Monroe, Louisiana. Dr. Stevens has served as a consultant to local, regional, and national firms for research projects, feasibility studies, and marketing planning, and has been a partner in a marketing research company. He also taught for ten years at Oral Roberts University where he was active in marketing projects for the university and ministry. Dr. Stevens is a member of the Southwestern Marketing Association, the Southern Marketing Association, and the Atlantic Marketing Association. He is the author of ten books and more than 80 articles on management, finance, and marketing.

David L. Loudon, PhD, is Professor of Marketing and Head of the Department of Management and Marketing in the College of Business Administration at Northeast Louisiana University in Monroe, Louisiana. He has conducted research in the United States, Europe, Asia, and Latin America on a variety of topics, including the application of marketing concepts to nontraditional areas. Dr. Loudon is a member of the Southwestern Marketing Association, the Southern Marketing Association, the Atlantic Marketing Association, and the American Marketing Association. He is the author of four books and numerous articles on management and marketing subjects.

Preface

This book is designed primarily for two groups of readers. The first is church administrators and pastors, and the second is leaders of para-church organizations, such as evangelists, foundation directors, and mission directors. This book could also serve as a supplemental text for college or seminary courses on church administration and planning.

We had three primary considerations when preparing this book. The first was length. We wanted to keep the amount of reading material brief enough to be read and reviewed quickly. We therefore had to omit many topics and provide only a limited discussion of others. The essential concepts and techniques are presented in a much more concise form.

The second consideration was to present material that was theoretically sound but practically oriented. We wanted the reader to be able to put the concepts presented to immediate use in decision making. We have also included worksheets at the end of each chapter to help readers develop their own strategic plans.

The final consideration was to provide a thorough set of appendixes to illustrate various aspects of strategic planning and a sample strategic plan. Thus, the reader not only can read about strategic planning but can actually see what one looks like. This is useful in evaluating plans prepared by others or in preparing your own.

The end result, we believe, is a book that is both readable and helpful to those involved with church/ministry administration. We hope the book will serve as both a tutorial and an easily accessible reference.

Acknowledgments

A book is seldom the work of the authors alone but involves the efforts of a great number of people. We would specifically like to thank the following individuals for their contributions: Melinda Calhoun, who tirelessly typed the final versions of the manuscript; Dr. Wade Paschal, Director of the Beeson Center for Biblical Preaching and Leadership at Asbury Theological Seminary, for the use of the Beeson Center's statement of purpose; Reverend Bob Clanton, for the use of the Monroe Covenant Church's statement of purpose; Bin Chi Zhang, Melissa Hewlett, and Sherry Stewart, students in the MBA program at Northeast Louisiana University, for their help in tracing references and gathering other materials; Carole Childress, of Leadership Network, who reviewed a final draft of the book; and finally, Gloria Honeycutt, for being the *perfect* secretary and for typing corrections of early manuscripts.

Chapter 1

Biblical Perspectives of Planning

Commit to the LORD whatever you do, and your plans will succeed.

−Proverbs 16:3

If you are struggling with any of the following problems or questions, this book, *Church and Ministry Strategic Planning,* may be very important to you.

> Why is there so much confusion among our associate pastors on what we are trying to accomplish?
> Why is there so much dissension and disagreement in this church?
> Why is there such a high turnover of people in our church, especially in leadership positions?
> Why did we build that building when it is not being used?
> As a pastor, why am I working 12 hours a day, and can never keep up?
> Why have we failed on a number of projects and missions?
> Why did God let us down?
> Why is the Devil stopping us?
> Why have the elders asked me to resign after everything I have put into this church or ministry?
> Why does this church lack enthusiasm?

If you are wrestling with one of these questions, the answer might be that your church or ministry lacks good long-term strategic planning. Part of strategic planning is the team-building approach of developing leaders and involving people in the plan.

PLANNING IS IMPORTANT

Planning as part of the management process is crucial to the success of any organization. This is especially true for the Church, although little research has been done on the relationship of planning to successful church ministry. Recently, however, an empirical study of the relationship between the use of the planning process and ministry effectiveness was conducted among senior pastors in one denomination. The study found that

- Larger churches (congregations of 250 or more) are more inclined to engage in written long-range planning;
- Most churches had been using long-range planning for less than three years and achieved attendance increases of 100 percent, twice the growth rate experienced by churches not using long-range planning;
- Ministry effectiveness was increased by the presence of written yearly and long-range plans;
- The lack of a written plan (yearly and/or long-range) hindered the ability of the church/pastor to be effective in ministering to the community.

The most important conclusion, according to the author of this research study, is that

> pastors and church leaders must be taught the importance of utilizing administration and management skills, especially planning, in the Church. They must also be given the tools necessary to incorporate planning into the ministries of the churches they serve. It is only through prayer and the use of the planning process that the Church, as an organization, can effectively fulfill the Great Commission that it has been given. (Burns 1992)

Of a large number of decisions made by a church or by an individual pastor there are a handful that can significantly impact the future of the church or pastor. These strategic decisions require careful identification and thoughtful consideration. This is the nature of the role of strategic planning.

Perspectives of strategic thinking can be illustrated with this question: Who are the two most important persons responsible for the success of an airplane's flight? Typical responses would be

- the pilot and the navigator,
- the pilot and the maintenance supervisor,
- the pilot and the air traffic controller, or
- the pilot and the flight engineer

All of these responses recognize the day-to-day hands-on importance of the pilot, and they all introduce one of several other important support or auxiliary functionaries to the answer. However, each of these segmented responses ignores the one person who is perhaps the single most important individual to the ultimate success of the airplane–the designer. The pilot and the designer are perhaps the two most important individuals to the success of an airplane: the pilot because of his day-to-day responsibilities in commanding the craft, and the designer because of his ability to create a concept that can be economically constructed, easily operated by any normally competent flight crew, and maintained safely by the ground crew.

Most contemporary pastors perceive themselves as the "pilot" of the church: taking off, landing, conferring with the navigator, and communicating with the air traffic controller. They generally view themselves as the chief hands-on operational manager. However, what has been most lacking in churches and ministries in the past few years has been an appreciation for the strategic viewpoint. There is a need for more emphasis on the "designer's" approach to operating a church or ministry. A well-conceived strategic planning system can facilitate this emphasis.

In a similar analogy, consider the illustration offered in the book, *The Master Builder* (Benjamin, Durkin, and Iverson 1985, 45) in which church strategic planning and flying are compared. The authors note that, before radios and instruments became common in small planes, pilots had to fly by visual flight rules. This meant that after take-off the plane had to be oriented in the right direction by some visual landmarks, perhaps a mountain that could be seen 50 miles out on the horizon. By keeping their eyes fixed on that landmark, the pilots could keep the plane steady and moving straight toward a long-range destination. A plane's magnetic compass needle would tend to sway, causing the plane to swerve back and forth in a wide zig-zag pattern. It could not provide steady direction because of its short-term gyrations. A pilot who tried to follow it strictly might never reach the destination, especially if fuel was limited.

This analogy clearly illustrates the difference between a short- and long-term perspective: one is choppy, erratic, and wastes fuel; the other guides the plane on a steady, constant, and certain course. A church without a long-term planning perspective faces the same situation. Instead of moving steadily toward God's goals, it will continually swerve off course due to the endless distractions that can prevent a church from pursuing God's purpose and vision. Thus, strategic planning is one of the keys to success of any undertaking and nowhere is it more important than in churches and ministries.

WHAT IS PLANNING?

Planning may be defined as a managerial activity which involves analyzing the environment, setting objectives, deciding on specific actions needed to reach the objectives, and also providing feedback on results. This process should be distinguished from the plan itself, which is a written document containing the results of the planning process; it is a written statement of what is to be done and how it is to be done. Planning is a continuous process which both precedes and follows other functions, in which plans are made and executed, and results are used to make new plans as the process continues.

TYPES OF PLANS

There are many types of plans but most can be categorized as *strategic* or *tactical*. Strategic plans cover a long period of time and may be referred to as a *long-term* plan. They are broad in scope and basically answer the question of how an organization is to commit its resources over the next five to ten years. Strategic plans are altered on an infrequent basis to reflect changes in the environment or overall direction of the ministry.

Tactical plans cover a short time period, usually a year or less. They are often referred to as *short-term* or *operational* plans. They specify what is to be done in a given year to move the organization toward its long-term objectives. In other words, what we do this year (short term) needs to be tied to where we want to be five to ten years in the future (long term).

Most churches and ministries which have been involved in planning have focused on short-term rather than long-term planning. Although this is better than not planning at all, it also means each year's plan is not related to anything long-term in nature and usually fails to move the organization to where it wants to be in the future.

Programs and events require planning. A ministry *program* is a large set of activities involving a whole area of a church's capabilities, such as planning for a church day school program. Planning for programs involves

1. dividing the total set of activities into meaningful parts;
2. assigning planning responsibility for each part to appropriate people;
3. assigning target dates for completion of plans;
4. determining and allocating the resources needed for each part.

Each major program or division within a church or ministry should have a strategic plan in place to provide a blueprint for the program over time.

A ministry *event* is generally of less scope and complexity. It is also not likely to be repeated on a regular basis. An event may be a part of a broader program or it may be self-contained. Even though it is a one-time event, planning is essential to accomplishing the objectives of the project and coordinating the activities which make up the event. A plan to have a "friend day" would be an example of a project plan.

ADVANTAGES OF PLANNING
FOR CHURCHES AND MINISTRIES

Why should a church or ministry devote time to planning? Consider the following questions:

Do you know where you are going and how you are going to get there?
Does everyone know what you are trying to accomplish?
Do all those involved know what is expected of them?

If the answer to any of these is no, then your church or ministry needs to develop a long-range plan with as many people involved as possible. Alvin J. Lindgren observed that

> most churches do not engage in such systematic long-range planning. Perhaps this is one reason why the church has not been able to reach and change society more effectively. Many churches operate on hand-to-mouth planning. They consider the pressing problems of the moment at each board meeting without placing them in proper perspective in relationship to either past or future. (1965, 226)

In many small churches, pastors may object to planning, thinking that it makes no sense for them, since theirs is only a small organization and everyone in the congregation knows what happened in the past year and what is likely to happen in the coming year. Another frequent objection is that there is no time for planning. A third is that there are not enough resources to allow for planning. All of these objections actually point out the necessity for planning even in the small church. Such an organization may actually have a sizeable budget, making it imperative to have a plan of where the church is heading. The observation that there is no time for planning may seem accurate, but this is probably due to the lack of planning in the past, which has left insufficient time for attention to such necessities. Finally, the argument that there are insufficient resources actually justifies the role of planning in order to obtain the maximum benefit from those resources being used in the church or ministry. Thus, planning is a critical element in any church's success.

Planning has many advantages. For example, it helps church or ministry administrators to adapt to changing environments, take advantage of opportunities created by change, reach agreements on major issues, and place responsibility more precisely. It also gives a sense of direction to staff members as well as providing a basis for gaining their commitment. The sense of vision that can be provided in a well-written plan also instills a sense of loyalty in church or ministry members or constituents.

A church can benefit from the planning process because this systematic, continuing process allows it to

1. assess the church's market position. This involves what is termed a SWOT analysis–examining the church's internal Strengths and Weaknesses and external Opportunities and Threats. Without explicit planning these elements may go unrecognized.
2. establish goals, objectives, priorities, and strategies to be completed within specified time periods. Planning will enable the church to assess accomplishment of the goals that are set and will help motivate staff and members to work together to achieve shared goals.
3. achieve greater staff and member commitment and teamwork aimed at meeting challenges and solving problems presented by changing conditions.
4. muster its resources to meet these changes through anticipation and preparation. "Adapt or die" is a very accurate admonition.

Pastors cannot control the future, but they should attempt to identify and isolate present actions and forecast how results can be expected to influence the future. The primary purpose of planning, then, is to ensure that current programs can be used to increase the chances of achieving future objectives and goals; that is, to increase the chances of making better decisions today that affect tomorrow's performance.

Unless planning leads to improved performance, it is not worthwhile. Thus, to have a church or ministry that looks forward to the future and tries to stay alive and prosper in a changing environment, there must be active, vigorous, continuous, and creative planning. Otherwise, a church will only react to its environment.

There are basically two reasons for planning: (1) protective benefits resulting from reduced chances for error in decision making, and (2) positive benefits, in the form of increased success in reaching ministry objectives.

Often, when pastors and churches plan poorly, they must constantly devote their energies to solving problems that would not have existed, or at least would be much less serious, with planning. They spend their time fighting fires rather than practicing fire prevention.

Long-range planning can become a means of renewal in the life of a congregation if the following points are remembered:

1. A unified purpose can be achieved only when all segments of the life of the church see themselves as part of a larger whole with a single goal;
2. Isolated individual decisions and commitments often influence future plans, even when they are not intended to do so;
3. When careful planning is lacking, groups in the church often become competitive and duplicate one another's work;
4. Without coordinated planning, groups in the church may come to feel they are ends in themselves and lose their sense of perspective in relation to the church;
5. Long-range planning is demanded by the magnitude of each church's task. (Lindgren 1965, 231)

PLANNING'S PLACE IN THE CHURCH OR MINISTRY

All pastors engage in planning to some degree. As a general rule, the larger the church becomes, the more the primary planning activities become associated with groups of people as opposed to individuals.

Many larger churches develop a planning committee or staff. Organizations set up such a planning group for one or more of the following reasons:

1. *Planning takes time.* A planning group can reduce the workload of individual staff or members.
2. *Planning takes coordination.* A planning group can help integrate and coordinate the planning activities of individual staff.
3. *Planning takes expertise.* A planning group can bring to a particular problem more tools and techniques than any single individual.

4. *Planning takes objectivity.* A planning group can take a broader view than one individual and go beyond specific projects and particular church departments.

A planning group generally has three basic areas of responsibility. First, it assists the pastor in developing goals, policies, and strategies for the church. The group facilitates the planning process by scanning and monitoring the church's environment. A second major responsibility of the group is to coordinate the planning of different levels and units within the church. Finally, the planning group acts as an organizational resource for pastors who lack expertise in planning.

In smaller churches, planning and execution must usually be carried out by the same people. The greatest challenge is to set aside time for planning in the midst of all the other day-to-day activities.

RESISTANCE TO THE PLANNING PROCESS

There are three main reasons why planning does not get done in churches and ministries today: (1) pastors and members lack training, (2) many perceive it as unscriptural, and (3) problems in implementation.

Lack of Management Training

The majority of churches in the United States have fewer than 200 active members, according to the data available from major denominations (Boyce 1984, 96). Most pastors have minimal management education and experience before entering active ministry and want to spend their time performing pastoral functions for which they are trained. Furthermore, few of these churches can or do draw on a pool of lay people with management training or skills. As such, the planning, objective setting, and other management functions are largely neglected.

Planning Is Thought to Be Unscriptural

Planning and objective setting of the strategic type have been largely neglected or purposely avoided by churches. This reluctance to plan stems from the fact that many view the application of strategic planning as inappropriate and unspiritual (Van Auken and Johnson 1984, 85). Some have felt that because churches are not businesses, they must not be managed as such: spiritual management is required for a spiritual organization. According to this view, church leaders are supposed to manage through God's perfect guidance and direction, to wait patiently for God to make things happen rather than "forcing things to happen." Furthermore, churches are admonished to strive for truly spiritual goals, not the numerical or quantifiable goals stressed in business (Myers 1983, 34).

Although planning has received more and more recognition for its applicability to churches, there are still some who doubt its worth to a religious organization.

> Many people are "Anti-planner," not just passively, but actively! . . . But once we begin to see that for the Christian, planning is making statements of faith about what God wants us to do and be, the Anti-planners may become converts. (Buckingham 1982, 1, 3)

For example, a pastor may be ridiculed by some for setting numeric goals, as this may not seem to be "religious." Often it is believed that the pastor is taking on the world's standards if he operates using business skills that have been applied to the secular world. But the same pastor may have no second thoughts about using the same type of sound system used by a business or even a rock band. A sound system is not good or bad in itself but rather the issue is how it is used. Planning which moves the church away from God's call is just bad planning; but planning as an activity is not bad in itself. The same can be said of money. The love of money is the root of all evil, not money itself.

A careful study of the Bible demonstrates the appropriateness and necessity for believers to plan their daily affairs. What does the Bible say about planning? We believe the Holy Spirit helps us know God's will and actions that are anointed. We do our best, then ask God for His best. Our spirit confirms when the right plan is in the will of God. Nothing in this book is meant to imply that the Lord is to be left out. Remember that a church's master plan should be the Master's plan for that church. Consider the following Bible verses:

Luke 14:28	Suppose one of you wants to build a tower. Will he not first sit down and estimate the cost to see if he has enough money to complete it?
1 Corinthians 14:40	But everything should be done in a fitting and orderly way.
Proverbs 16:3	Commit to the Lord whatever you do, and your plans will succeed.
Proverbs 16:9	In his heart a man plans his course, but the Lord determines his steps.
Psalm 20:4	May he give you the desire of your heart and make all your plans succeed.
Colossians 3:23	Whatever you do, work at it with all your heart, as working for the Lord, not for men.
Proverbs 15:22	Plans fail for lack of counsel, but with many advisers they succeed.
Proverbs 20:5	The purposes of a man's heart are deep waters, but a man of understanding draws them out.
Proverbs 24:3	By wisdom a house is built, and through understanding it is established.
1 Corinthians 14:33	For God is not a God of disorder but of peace.

In Appendix A we provide an extensive list of Bible verses related to planning.

Implementation Problems

Although there is much academic and theoretical support for planning, the actual implementation of it often runs aground on the shores of ministry reality. Even among very progressive churches you find significant resistance to planning. Some of the most common arguments against it are:

1. planning is not action oriented;
2. planning takes too much time, we are too busy to plan;
3. planning is unrealistic because of the rapid change in our environment (demographics, etc.);
4. planning becomes an end, not just a means to an end.

Many of these arguments stem from the same kind of thinking that would rank the pilot as the most important person in the success of an airplane. To be helpful, planning does not depend on complete forecasting accuracy. In fact, a variety of futuristic alternatives or scenarios can be very helpful in establishing planning parameters. Often a best-, most-likely-, and worst-case approach is used. This three-level forecast gives dimension to the process of recognizing, anticipating, and managing change.

The objection that planning is not "hands-on" and related to the important day-to-day operations of the church is frequent. However, this point of view is shortsighted in terms of long-term success. Planning is not just for dreamers, in fact, it lets the church administrative team determine what can be done today to accomplish or avoid some future circumstance.

Planning sometimes becomes an end in the minds of some users. This is particularly true when planning is solely a committee responsibility within a church. A committee staff can facilitate the strategic planning process, but the process will not be a dynamic life-blood activity of the organization without the ongoing involvement of the pastor and staff members. President Eisenhower has been widely quoted as saying, "Plans are nothing, planning is everything." The trust he expressed was that the actual plan itself was not the end, but that the process of planning–developing futuristic scenarios, evaluating the environment and competition, assessing internal strengths and capabilities, revising objectives and tactics–was the organization dialogue that was most important. This church dialogue ideally breaks down barriers to communication, exposes blind spots, tests logic, measures the environment, and determines feasibility. The end result is more effective and efficient implementation of ministry activity.

Yet, the advantages of planning far outweigh any of these and other perceived disadvantages. Planning not only should be done but must be done.

THE GREATEST NEEDS OF TODAY'S MINISTRIES AND CHURCHES

In our own informal surveys both denominational and nondenominational pastors appeared to be unanimous in their beliefs that strategic planning is important. To put matters into perspective, let us try to translate church and ministry success into a formula:

$$X = f(A,B,C,D,E,F,G,H,I \ldots)$$

In this case X is success for the church or ministry, a dependent variable, and is on the left side of the equation. The = sign means a balance, or equal to what is on the other side; the f means "a function of." On the right side are all the independent variables that affect success:

A. pastor as spiritual leader
B. pastor as manager
C. planning system
D. organization system
E. control system
F. needs of people met
G. denomination's national influence
H. denomination's local influence
 I. location
    etc.

Only a few independent variables are listed, but the possibilities are endless. Notice that success is not necessarily equated to size. We are defining success in broader terms than church members, budget, and so forth. There seems to be a widespread notion that size is the only barometer, but we do not hold that belief.

God has raised up many spiritual leaders. We believe the greatest problems holding back these leaders–and the churches and ministries they serve–involve some combination of independent variables B, C, D, and E. Management, planning, organization, and control are some of the greatest needs of churches and ministries today.

We assume that every pastor is to some degree a spiritual leader, or he could not remain in the pulpit. However, his entire ministry and the success of his church are in direct proportion to variables B, C, D, and E. If you assume all other variables are constant and full effort goes into B, C, D, and E, then the X factor (success), the dependent variable, has to increase. Without training and knowledge in the area of planning and management, the church and ministry have a ceiling on success. No organization can get any bigger than the capacity of its managers to manage. The hindrance is not the needs of the people, for needs are always there. It is not the denomination or location, it is plainly management, planning, organization, and control.

If pastors and evangelists could improve each of these areas just a little each year, they would be much more successful. They could drastically reduce all the obvious errors in direction, false starts, dissipated efforts, frustrated staff members, and waste. The religious world is ripe for criticism by almost anyone looking for waste and inefficiency.

Christians should not wait until someone comes along and creates a big scandal about waste and inefficiency. We need to put our shoulders to the wheel and pay attention to management, planning, organization, control, and people. If we do not, on the whole, the church will accomplish in the next 50 years about what it did in the last 50 years–it will maintain the status quo.

Our observation is that many people in ministry and church work are reluctant to plan, do not want a plan in writing, and do not ask for advice. The tendency is to be led by "the Spirit," which is sometimes a whim or emotional impulse. This reflects our general American inclination to "hang loose." Probably 75 percent of the profit-making organizations that we have observed or worked with have the same problem. The 25 percent that have the discipline to plan and manage properly far outperform those that do not. Higher profits, better service, and lower turnover are but a few of the rewards. The same good fortune comes to those ministries and churches that have the discipline to plan and manage properly.

Many times Christians say "The Devil is fighting us" when a plan or project goes sour. We are not discounting a demon force, but in many instances the Devil does not need to fight Christians. Could it be that we hold ourselves back? The Devil can sleep late and rest while we run around in circles. He does not need to work hard. We are our own worst enemies. Many church or ministry failures can be traced to poor planning, lack of getting people involved in the planning, and generally poor management. We often sense a spirit of extreme urgency in church ministry planning. This is used as a "go for it–if it is of the Lord, it will prosper" mentality. What is the rush? Many churches and ministries need to slow down, plan, and pray. Often they have rushed around in circles for the past few years. We do not believe God will give His best until we give our best. Included in doing our best is using the best planning and management philosophies and techniques available.

The need for the performance of managerial functions in churches in order for them to be more effective ministerially has long been recognized. Vast social questions and complex conditions in almost every community emphasize the need for good management in churches (Hale 1984, 30).

Where planning in churches occurs without quantitative goals which are clearly understood and widely supported, vigorous progress is unlikely and probably impossible. The importance of setting goals is to provide direction and unity of purpose, but it must be the congregation's goal, as it is not the planners but the congregation that will ensure the plan's success. However, a balance should be struck and the two mistakes of planning extremes, those of asking the congregation to do either all the thinking or none, must be avoided. Planning is important to bring these objectives to fruition. This is not easy, but the alternative is for the church to be tossed to and fro, buffeted by every unforeseen circumstance, and blown off course (Gray 1983).

We see creative planning as the church's hope for the future. Visionary thinking, solid purpose, or long-range dreams should be first in the basic concern of the church ministry. In a society where many institutions are becoming stagnant, it is imperative that churches have an expanding vision. Church planning has never been met with much enthusiasm. Even in larger churches, the enthusiasm for a plan seldom extends beyond a year unless it involves a new building. No matter how misunderstood and poorly appreciated planning is, it is a major factor in sharing the hope for the world–the gospel of Christ (McDonough 1975, 5).

Every pastor needs a vision or a dream. Mission statements and dreams are the vessels through which your desires are fulfilled. Without a specific goal, a vision is no vision.

SUMMARY

We have attempted to establish in this chapter our belief that (1) methods used successfully in industry are applicable to churches and ministries; (2) there is a place for better planning and management; (3) many pastors do believe that there is a need for planning; (4) most of the identifiable failures cannot be blamed on the Devil; and (5) the Bible supports, overall, a growing sense of the planning concept.

The philosophy of this book is that in order for everyone in the church or ministry–the elders, the pastor, the congregation–to be successful, a strategic plan is desperately needed. If you look at the mistakes of the past, it is obvious that many churches and ministries have followed the zig-zag flight pattern described earlier. Over years of consulting with churches and ministries, the authors have observed this exact pattern again and again. If you take the time and effort to study this book, follow up on your people, apply the format prescribed here, and prayerfully keep God in every step of the plan, here is what we believe you can expect:

1. A sense of enthusiasm in your church or ministry
2. A five-year plan in writing to which everyone is committed
3. A sense of commitment by the entire church to its overall direction
4. Clear job duties and responsibilities
5. Time for the leaders to do what they have been called to do
6. Clear and evident improvement in the health and vitality of every member of the church staff

7. Measurable improvement in the personal lives of all those in responsible positions with time for vacations, family, and personal pursuits
8. The ability to measure very specifically the growth and contribution made by senior pastors or evangelists at the close of their careers
9. Guaranteed leadership of the church or ministry because a plan is in place in writing and is understood–even more importantly, a management team and philosophy will be in place to guide the church or ministry into its next era of growth

In the next chapter we present an overview of the entire strategic planning process; in Appendix B we also provide an outline of a strategic plan. Then, in the following chapters, we cover each step of the planning process. We explain the theory behind each step, and give actual examples to help you to understand that step. Make notes on your own situation as you read. Read on with excitement.

Chapter 2

Overview of Strategic Planning

But everything should be done in a fitting and orderly way.

–I Cor. 14:40

In this chapter we present an overview of the strategic planning process. Each of the areas discussed are examined in more detail in later chapters. Our intention here is to provide an introduction to the major components of the process.

WHAT IS STRATEGIC PLANNING?

The word strategic means "pertaining to strategy." Strategy is derived from the Greek word, *strategia*, which means generalship, art of the general, or, more broadly, leadership. The word strategic, when used in the context of planning, provides a perspective to planning which is long run in nature and deals with achieving specified end results. Just as military strategy has as its objective the winning of the war, so, too, strategic planning has as its objective the achievement of ministry goals–the winning of the lost and the equipping of the saints.

Strategic decisions must be differentiated from tactical decisions. The strategic decisions outline the overall game plan or approach, while the tactical decisions involve implementing various activities which are necessary to carry out a strategy. For example, a church which decides to change locations because of shifting population trends and industrial development around its present location is making strategic decisions. Then many other decisions must be made about the exact location, size of the building, parking facilities, etc. These all have long-term implications and are therefore strategic in nature. Other decisions such as wall colors, decor, and air conditioning must then be made. These are tactical decisions needed to carry out or implement the previous strategic decision. Thus, the strategic decision provides the overall framework within which the tactical decisions are made. It is critically important that pastors are able to differentiate between these types of decisions to identify whether the decision has short- or long-term implications.

THE STRATEGIC PLANNING PROCESS

The strategic planning process is basically a matching process involving ministry resources and opportunities. The objective of this process is to peer through the "strategic window" (an opportunity that will not always be there) and identify opportunities which the individual church or ministry is equipped to take advantage of or respond to. Thus the strategic management process can be defined as a managerial process which involves matching ministry capabilities to ministry opportunities. These opportunities are created over time and decisions revolve around investing or divesting resources to address these opportunities. The context in which these strategic decisions are made is (1) the church or ministry operating environment, (2) ministry purpose or mission, and (3) objectives. This overall process is depicted in Exhibit 2-1. Strategic planning is the process which ties all these elements together to facilitate strategic choices which are consistent with all three areas and then implements and evaluates these choices. Appendix A presents an outline of a strategic plan.

The successful results of planning described earlier can be achieved through implementing an effective strategic planning process. The following breakdown of this process is a complete outline of the system capable of creating true change in ministry attitudes as well as in productivity. Such a philosophy involves

1. defining a ministry purpose and reason for being;
2. analyzing the environment in which it operates, realistically assessing its strengths and weaknesses, and making assumptions about unpredictable future events;

3. prescribing written, specific, and measurable objectives in principal result areas contributing to the church or ministry's purpose;
4. developing strategies on how to use available resources to reach objectives;
5. developing operational plans to meet objectives including establishing individual objectives and strategies;
6. evaluating performance to determine whether it is keeping pace with attainment of objectives and is consistent with defined purpose and changing objectives, strategies, or operational plans in light of the evaluation.

It is important to recognize at this point what we call "the two Ps." The first P means Product: get the plan in writing. The plan must be something you can hold in your hand, a written product of your efforts. If the plan is not in writing, it is called daydreaming. When it is in writing, you are indicating to yourself and others that you are serious about it. The second P represents Process: every plan must have maximum input from everyone. Those who execute the plan must be involved in construction of the plan. The Bible tells us to obtain input. Note the following three Scripture verses:

> Without counsel purposes are disappointed: but in the multitude of counsellors they are established (*Proverbs 18:22*).

> Hear counsel, and receive instruction, that thou mayest be wise in thy latter end (*Proverbs 19:20*).

> Every purpose is established by counsel (*Proverbs 20:18*).

The best way to ensure a plan's failure is to overlook both the product and the process. They are equally important.

While there are many different ways in which a church or ministry could approach the strategic planning process, a systematic approach that carries the organization through a series of integral steps helps to focus attention on a basic set of questions each organization must answer:

1. *What will we do?* This question focuses attention on the specific needs the church or ministry will try to meet.

2. *Who will we do it for?* This question addresses the need for a church or ministry to identify the various groups whose needs will be met.
3. *How will we do what we want to do?* Answering this question forces the organization to think about the many avenues through which ministry may be channeled.

The strategic planning process used by an organization must force church/ministry leadership to deal with these questions on a continuous basis. The organization evolves over time into what God has established it to be, to do the work that only it can do.

Strategic planning involves the following steps:

1. defining an organization's purpose and reason for being;
2. analyzing the environment, assessing its strengths and weaknesses, and making assumptions;
3. prescribing written, specific, and measurable objectives in the principal result areas that contribute to the organization's purpose;
4. developing strategies on how to use available resources to meet objectives;
5. developing operational plans to meet objectives including plans for all individuals in the organization;
6. setting up control and evaluation procedures to determine if performance is keeping pace with attainment of objectives and if it is consistent with defined purpose.

The six steps of the strategic planning process, as illustrated in Exhibit 2-1, are important because they force the organization to consider certain questions. As each step requires the people at various organizational levels to discuss, study, and negotiate, the process as a whole fosters a planning mentality. When the six steps are complete, the end result is a strategic plan for the organization specifying why the organization exists, what it is trying to accomplish, and how resources will be utilized to accomplish objectives and fulfill its purpose.

EXHIBIT 2-1

Strategic Planning Process

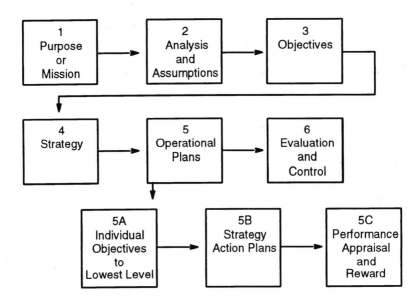

Defining Purpose

The first and probably the most important consideration when developing a strategic plan is to define the purpose, mission, or the "reason for being" of the organization or any specific part of it. This is usually a difficult process even though it may appear simple. For example, a church or ministry which defines itself as a "group of believers who proclaim the Gospel" may be on the right track but will constantly face the need to explain and expand this definition. Does proclaim mean preach and preach only or does it also include teaching? If teaching is added to the definition, will that involve teaching of spiritual concepts only or would other educational needs be addressed such as preschool, church school, even Bible college or an institution of higher learning? Granted, these things may change as the organization evolves and grows; but thinking through these issues provides a sense of vision and also prevents the church or ministry from engaging in activities which do not fit with what the organization wants to do or be.

Members should try to visualize what they want the organization to become, and should incorporate this dream or vision into their purpose statement. If they can see where they are going and have an image of the real mission of the organization, their plans will fall into place more easily.

The Bible explicitly admonishes us to have a dream and vision. For example, consider the following: Where there is no vision, the people perish (*Proverbs 29:18*). Your old men shall dream dreams, your young men shall see visions (*Joel 2:28*). A vision of what can be accomplished creates the spark and energy for the whole planning and management process. It is important to spend ample time defining this purpose statement. The process should emphasize involving everyone in the dream of how things can be. Without a vision, people just work day-to-day and tend not to be as productive or willing to expend effort.

A good statement of purpose not only clarifies what the church does, it sets boundaries. It defines what the church will not do. It helps limit expectations, and that alone can make it the pastor's best friend (Shelly 1985/86).

Analysis and Assumptions

It is vital for the church to gauge the environment within which it operates. This should be standard practice for all churches. The only way we can manage change is to constantly monitor the environment within which we operate. This analysis stage is where we look at the external environment, internal strengths and weaknesses, and potential threats and opportunities.

For example, many "downtown" churches have faced a dilemma of whether to remain in the downtown area or move to the suburbs. One church found that its historic location resulted in two significant problems: lack of space to grow and a change in the socioeconomic makeup of the neighborhood. The socioeconomic changes made the church ineffective in meeting the needs of those in the neighborhood who were of different ethnic backgrounds and also made it difficult to attract younger couples into the church.

This church's solution was quite interesting. Members raised funds to buy land and build a new church in a growing part of the community, and the conference put a new minister in the old church of the same ethnic background as those in the neighborhood. Everybody won! The old neighborhood church could serve the needs of those who lived there with a great physical plant that included a gym, while the new church was built in an area where there was no church of that denomination and it too grew and prospered.

Many organizations have found it useful to use an analysis framework referred to earlier as a SWOT analysis. SWOT is an acronym for strengths, weaknesses, opportunities, and threats: strengths and weaknesses refer to elements internal to the organization, while opportunities and threats are external to the organization. A detailed SWOT analysis helps the church/ministry take a good look at the organization's favorable and unfavorable factors with a view toward building on strengths and eliminating or minimizing weaknesses. At the same time, leadership of a church or ministry must also access external opportunities which could be pursued and threats which must be dealt with in order for the church to survive.

The next stage is to state your major assumptions about spheres over which you have little or absolutely no control, such as the external environment. One good place to start is to extend some of the items studied in the external analysis. Should this stage appear relatively unimportant in developing a strategic plan, consider that by not making explicit assumptions you are making one major implicit assumption–things are going to remain the same and nothing that happens is important enough to affect you!

Establishing Objectives

Often the words "key results," "goals," and "targets" are used synonymously with objectives when thinking about long- and short-term objectives. Think of an archer drawing an arrow and aiming directly at a target. The bull's-eye represents exactly where you want to be at a certain point in time. A pastor wants the whole church aimed at the same target just as an archer wants the arrow aimed at the target. At the other extreme, an archer who shoots arrows off in any direction is liable to hit almost anything–including the wrong target. People get confused and disorganized if they do not know where they are going.

Objectives must be clear, concise, written statements outlining what is to be accomplished in key priority areas, over a certain time period, in measurable terms that are consistent with the overall purpose of the organization. Objectives can be classified as routine, problem-solving, innovative, team, personal, or budget performance. Objectives do not determine the future, but they are the means by which the resources and energies are mobilized for the making of the future.

Objectives are the results desired upon completion of the planning period. In the absence of objectives, no sense of direction can be attained in decision making. In other words, if you don't know where you are going, any road will take you there. In planning, objectives answer one of the basic questions posed in the planning process: Where do we want to go? These objectives become the focal point for strategy decisions.

Another basic purpose served by objectives is in the evaluation of performance. Objectives in the strategic plan become the yardsticks used for this evaluation. It is impossible to evaluate performance without some standard against which results can be compared. The objectives become the standards for evaluation because they are the statement of results desired by the planner.

Strategy Development

After developing a set of objectives for the time period covered by the strategic plan, a strategy to accomplish those objectives must be formulated. An overall strategy must first be designed; then the operational strategies must be developed.

Strategy alternatives are the alternate courses of action evaluated by management before commitment is made to a specific option outlined in the strategic plan. Thus, strategy is the link between objectives and results.

Operational Plans

After all the steps have been taken and a strategy has been developed to meet your objectives and goals, it is time to develop an operational or action plan. The operational plan stage is the "action" or "doing" stage. Here you hire, fire, build, advertise, and so on. How many times has a group of people planned something, gotten enthusiastic, and then nothing happened? This is usually because they did not complete an operational or action plan to implement their strategy.

Operational plans must be developed for all the areas that are used to support the overall strategy. These include production, communication, finance, and staffing. Each of these more detailed plans is designed to spell out what needs to happen in a given area to implement the strategic plan.

Supporting the operational plans are the individual plans of all members of the organization. These are shown as steps 5A, 5B, and 5C in Exhibit 2-1. When planning is carried from the top to the lowest level in the organization, everyone becomes involved in setting and negotiating personal objectives which support the organization's objectives. Then each person begins to develop an individual action plan which is used to accomplish these personal objectives. Finally, the personal performance appraisal which must be done on an individual basis uses those individual objectives as the basis of appraisal and reward.

Evaluation and Control

Failure to establish procedures to appraise and control the strategic plan can lead to less than optimal performance. A plan is not complete until the controls are identified, and the procedures for recording and transmitting control information to the administrators of the plan are established. Many organizations fail to understand the importance of establishing procedures to appraise and control the planning process. Control should be a natural follow-through in developing a plan.

Planning and control should be integral processes. The strategic planning process results in a strategic plan. This plan is implemented (activities are performed in the manner described in the plan) and results are produced. These results are attendance, baptisms, contributions, and accompanying constituent attitudes, behaviors, etc. Information on these and other key result areas is given to administrators, who compare the results with objectives to evaluate performance. This performance evaluation identifies the areas where decisions must be made to adjust activities, people, or finances. The actual decision making controls the plan by altering it to accomplish stated objectives, and a new cycle begins.

Individual performance appraisal is a vital part of this step. Rewards or reprimands must be related to the personal achievement or lack of achievement of agreed-upon objectives. This creates a work environment where people know what to do and rewards are tied to performance.

STRATEGIC PLANNING AS A PROCESS

The word process refers to a series of actions directed to an end. The actions are the activities in which the church or ministry engages to accomplish objectives and fulfill its mission. There are several important reasons for viewing strategic planning as a process. First, a change in any component of the process will affect most or all of the other components. For example, a change in purpose or objective will lead to new analysis, strategies, and evaluations. Thus, major changes which affect the organization must lead to a reevaluation of all the elements of the plan.

A second reason for viewing strategic planning as a process is that a process can be studied and improved. A church or ministry just getting involved in strategic planning will need to review the whole process on an annual basis not only to account for changing environmental forces but to improve or refine the plan. Purpose statements, objectives, strategies, and appraisal techniques can be fine tuned over time as the planners gain more experience and as new and better information becomes available.

Finally and perhaps most importantly, involvement in the strategic planning process can become the vehicle through which the whole organization mobilizes its energies to accomplish its purpose. If all members of the organization can participate in the process in some way, an atmosphere can be created within the organization that implies that doing the right things and doing things right is everybody's job. Participation instills ownership. It's not "my plan" or "their plan" but "God's plan" that becomes important; and everyone will *want* to make a contribution to make it happen.

STRATEGY IMPLEMENTATION

The focus of this book is on the strategic planning process which results in the development of a strategic plan. This plan becomes the blueprint for carrying out the many activities in which a church or ministry is involved. There are many other issues that determine the effectiveness of an organization which are beyond the scope of this book. These issues essentially revolve around implementing the strategic plan through (1) staffing and training personnel and volunteers, (2) developing organizational relationships among staff/volunteers, (3) achieving commitment, (4) developing a positive organizational culture, (5) leadership styles, and (6) personnel evaluation and reward systems.

Our lack of discussion of these topics is due to space limitation and a desire to keep the length of the book manageable for readers. While the scriptures state that "where there is no vision, the people perish" (*KJV, Proverbs 29:8*) it is also true that without people, especially the right people, the vision will perish. Both effective planning and implementation are needed to create an effective organization. The strategic plan concentrates on "doing the right things" while implementation concentrates on "doing things right." An example of an entire strategic plan for a ministry is presented in Appendix C.

SUMMARY

In this chapter we have presented an overview of the strategic planning process in which a series of thought-provoking questions must be answered. The process is a set of integral steps which carries the planners through a sequence that involves providing answers to these questions and then continually rethinking and reevaluating these answers as the organization and its environment change.

A helpful tool at this stage is the Planning and Management Systems Audit form provided in Appendix D. This form, when thoughtfully filled out, will provide an assessment of your current position in terms of planning and management of your organization. It will help point out where to direct your efforts to improve the efficiency and effectiveness of the organization God has entrusted to your leadership.

PLANNING PROCESS WORKSHEET

This worksheet is provided to aid your church or ministry in starting the strategic planning process.

1. Who should be involved in the planning process?

_____

_____

_____

_____

2. Where will planning sessions be held?

_____

_____

_____

_____

3. When will planning sessions be held?

_____

_____

_____

4. What types of background material do participants need prior to starting the first session?

_____

_____

_____

5. Who will lead the process? Who will ultimately be responsible for arranging sessions, getting material typed, reproduced, and distributed?

_____

_____

_____

6. When and how will members of the staff, board, congregation, or others be involved in the process?

_____

_____

_____

7. How will the results be communicated to everyone in the organization?

_____

_____

_____

8. Who will train/supervise staff members in working with their own staff and volunteers in setting objectives, developing action plans, and performance appraisals?

_____

_____

_____

9. How frequently will the process be reviewed and by whom?

_____

_____

_____

10. Who will be responsible for dealing with external groups (Bishops, media people, consultants) in preparing the plan?

_____

_____

_____

Chapter 3

Defining Your Purpose

Where there is no vision, the people perish. (*KJV*)

—Proverbs 29:8

This chapter outlines the first step in the strategic planning process. Without a clear and carefully considered statement of purpose all other stages of the process will be misguided. We will therefore discuss the value of defining the ministry's purpose, describe how to write effective statements of purpose or mission, and present two examples of mission statements.

THE IMPORTANCE OF DEFINING PURPOSE

The first and probably most important consideration when developing a strategic plan is to define the purpose, mission, or "reason for being" for the organization or any specific part of it. This is usually a difficult process. Peter Drucker, a management consultant and writer, has led the way in stressing the importance of defining purpose. An organization develops to satisfy a need in the marketplace. Drucker states that the organization's purpose is defined by the want the customer satisfies by buying a product or service. Thus, satisfying the customer is the mission and purpose of every business (1974, 79). Organizations need a clear definition of purpose and mission. This raises the questions "What is our purpose," and "What should it be?" Drucker's answer is that only a clear definition of the mission and purpose of the business makes possible clear and realistic business objectives. It is the foundation for priorities, strategies, plans, and work assignments. It is the starting point for the design of managerial structure and jobs (1974, 75).

Clearly, if purpose is defined casually or introspectively, or if the list of key result areas neglects some of the less obvious threats and opportunities, the organization is at risk. As Calvin Coolidge put it: "No enterprise can exist for itself alone. It ministers to some great need, it performs some great service not for itself but for others; or failing therein it ceases to be profitable and ceases to exist."

It is in this purpose statement that the vision and the dream for the church or ministry must be reflected. This purpose statement sets the stage for all planning. Objectives, which are covered later in the text, must by their very nature contribute to achieving what is in the purpose statement. In a study of private Christian college and university administrations, it was discovered that all those surveyed had a purpose and mission statement, but only 50 percent had specific measurable objectives of what was to be accomplished.

A mission statement aids a church or ministry by

1. giving it a reason for being, and an explanation to members and others as to why it exists as an organization;
2. helping to place boundaries around the ministry and thus defining what it will and will not do;
3. describing the need the organization is attempting to meet in the world;
4. giving a general description of how the organization is going to respond to that need;
5. acting as the hook on which the primary objectives of the organization can be hung;
6. helping to form the basis for the ethos (or culture) of the organization;
7. helping to communicate to those outside what the organization is all about ("Defining the Mission" 1984, 1, 2).

WRITING A STATEMENT OF PURPOSE

The following list (Lambert 1975, 28) provides several helpful tips on writing and evaluating a purpose statement.

1. Identify the mission of that part of the organization to which the group is accountable. A parish council may be accountable

to the parish at large, the pastor, bishop, diocesan pastoral council, or all of these. The liturgy committee will be accountable to the parish council. The director of religious education may be accountable to the religious education committee, pastor, or both.

2. Determine that portion of the above mission statement for which the group is responsible. While the parish council is accountable for the total parish operation, the maintenance committee, for example, will be responsible only for that portion of the parish council's mission that deals with maintaining the grounds and buildings in a usable and functional state.

3. Prepare a rough draft of the mission statement which covers the purpose of the group and the major activities it performs. With a working team, such as a parish staff or parish council, a rough draft mission statement can be developed at an all-day meeting, using an outside facilitator who is familiar with communications techniques, group processes, and the concept of mission statements. The meeting can begin with each individual writing a version of the mission statement on newsprint. When these drafts are all assembled, the group can review each one for clarity and understanding. Finally, consolidate those portions that are similar so that only areas of wide disagreement are left. At this point, negotiations can be carried out between members of the group until there is general agreement on all points. The final result is the rough draft of the mission statement.

A purpose statement must be built around several points:

1. *Congregational Care*–typically this includes corporate worship, administration of the sacraments, pastoral care, fellowship, and the nurturing, education, and training for Christian discipleship of the members.

2. *Outreach and Evangelism*–this part of the statement focuses on the imperative to go out and confront individuals outside the church with the good news that Jesus Christ is their Redeemer and Savior. While the first part of this outline was directed toward the parish's ministry to persons inside the

gathered community, this part emphasizes the parish's responsibility to individuals outside the church.

3. *Witness and Mission*–the emphasis here is on the church's responsibility to be a living witness for Christ to the groups, organizations, structures, and institutions outside the church in the world. This also helps the members to understand both the legitimacy and the imperative for the parish's involvement in the social, economic, and political issues in the local community. (Schaller 1965, 33)

SAMPLE MISSION STATEMENTS

It might be helpful at this point to examine a mission statement prepared by a church and a ministry. Note that these statements reflect the uniqueness of the organizations in terms of their reason for being and also serve as guidelines for what the organization should be doing. These statements were developed through a process involving many people and over a period of six to eight months. Initial statements were revised many times to add specificity and clarity to the terms used to define purpose.

Mission Statement
Monroe Covenant Church
Monroe, Louisiana

Statement of Purpose

Monroe Covenant Church is a full-gospel (charismatic), interdenominational congregation deeply rooted in the historic evangelical faith. Our basic purpose is to (1) glorify and please God, (2) edify and train believers, and (3) evangelize and saturate the world with the Gospel of Jesus Christ. Our emphasis is on the three "Bs": Believing, Becoming, and Belonging.

Believing

We are a church that believes that our duty is to:

1. bring people to a saving knowledge of Jesus Christ as the only way to salvation;
2. help people experience the Baptism in the Holy Spirit with all His gifts and fruits;
3. train Christians to share their faith with others and to proclaim the Gospel;
4. do the compassionate and powerful works of Christ in the world;
5. give practical application to our Christian faith in the areas of (1) family life, (2) church life, (3) job, (4) ethics, (5) morality, (6) personal relationships, (7) financial integrity, (8) civic responsibility, and (9) community involvement;
6. seek ways to build the unity of the Church by recognizing and relating with individuals and Churches outside our local congregation, and in so doing identify with and incorporate into the larger Church in our city, state, and the Church Universal.

Becoming

We are a church that desires to:

1. increase in the knowledge and power of (1) God's Word, (2) prayer, and (3) fellowship with believers, according to Acts 2:42;
2. grow in our ability to worship God personally and corporately;
3. grow in our commitment to the Lord as expressed in our loyalty, faithfulness, obedience, integrity, and love;
4. grow in individual and corporate freedom in Christ by using all the means of grace, among which are healing, counseling, deliverance, and forgiveness, to be Christians who then might be able to help others also enter that same freedom in Christ;
5. increase in making a difference for the Kingdom of God in our society.

Belonging

We are a church that emphasizes belonging by:

1. committing to work out practical Christian relationships according to the "one another" passages of the New Testament,

and, in so doing, to the best of our understanding fulfill what the Bible describes as covenant love and covenant relationship;

2. teaching, identifying, training, recognizing, and releasing the many diverse gifts in the Body of Christ so that believers better find and function in their God-given places;
3. caring for the many diverse needs of the individual members of the church;
4. attitudes and actions of friendliness and acceptance so that everyone will know that we care for them.

Mission Statement
Beeson Center for Biblical Preaching and Pastoral Leadership
Asbury Theological Seminary
Wilmore, Kentucky

Our Mission

The Beeson Center for Biblical Preaching and Pastoral Leadership exists to serve the church through serving pastors. Our purpose is the advanced training of pastors in preaching and leadership skills for the sake of Christ, to increase the effectiveness of their ministry, and to equip God's people under the authority of scripture and in obedience to the call for scriptural holiness and love.

Our Message

The Beeson Center for Biblical Preaching and Pastoral Leadership is committed to the following expression of this purpose.

1. Faithful proclamation of the Word of God is the foundation of ministry. Faithful proclamation begins with faithful pastors who experience and understand the truth of God's word in their own lives. Effective preaching requires rightly interpreting scripture. Effective communication implies not only speaking the truth, but speaking in terms which can be understood and appropriated by the culture in which we live. The Beeson Center exists to train pastors to better understand and

communicate the gospel as teachers, preachers, and models of the Word of God.

2. Worship forms and energizes the community of God. The Word proclaimed by the preacher does not exist in isolation, but in the totality of worship which communicates the gospel on many levels. The Beeson Center exists to foster the creative integration of proclamation into overall worship in terms which honor God and speak to our times.

3. Every church, informed by Biblical mandates such as the Great Commission, must form its own vision. Each pastor should articulate a personal vision and call. Pastors and churches have individual gifts that function best when applied to appropriate missions. The Beeson Center exists to foster the pastor's understanding of his or her own gifts and call, and to develop a vision for the church they serve.

4. The church today exists in a world which is defined and formed by the growing power of media and technology. Each generation throughout church history has learned to use the technological tools of its day in the service of Christ. The Beeson Center is committed to the integration of excellent media and computer technology in the communication of the gospel of Christ.

5. The ministry of the church consists of the work of all Christians as they are faithful to Christ. The pastor is called to equip and train the whole people of God for this ministry. The Beeson Center exists to provide training and guidance for pastors in the development of staff and lay ministry.

Our Market

1. The Beeson Center for Biblical Preaching and Pastoral Leadership at Asbury Theological Seminary begins with its base in the Wesleyan-Holiness and Methodist traditions of Christianity. We seek first to reach and to serve pastors in this tradition from the historic perspective of the seminary.

2. We seek to be inclusive, serving both those women and men from all races who form our historic constituencies, and also pastors and churches from other theological traditions. We seek to focus our service for young pastors of promise primar-

ily through a year-long program in Biblical preaching and pastoral leadership. We seek to focus our service to established pastors primarily through short-term, intensive programs in specific aspects of teaching and leadership.
3. We seek to serve the church-at-large through research, publications, and media instruction.

Our Measures for Our Future

1. The Beeson Center will incorporate through the existing Doctor of Ministry program a one-year, on-site DMin program in Biblical Preaching and Leadership which will be funded by the Beeson Scholars Program and housed in the Beeson Center. We seek, by 1993, to have 12 scholars on campus, and 24 by 1995. This program will concentrate on pastors early in their career who show unusual promise as preachers and leaders for the future of the church.
2. The Beeson Center will establish the Senior pastor Program of short-term study opportunities for established pastors. The program will offer intensive study and training opportunities in preaching, theological and spiritual formation, leadership, church administration, and programming for active senior pastors. We would like to have 40 pastors involved by 1993 and 80 by 1995.
3. The Beeson Center will establish a research and publicity program–beginning with a journal or newsletter on preaching and leadership in 1992.
4. The Beeson Center is committed to the use of advanced technology and media resources in teaching and for the use of the church. The Beeson Center will develop a system of optic fiber communication within the Asbury Theological Seminary campus to promote the use of media and technology for teaching in classroom settings. The Center will also promote the development of video instructional resources for pastors and churches, concentrating on preaching, worship, church programs, and related issues. The Center will develop the ability to offer teaching programs to pastors and churches through satellite relay for instruction away from the Wilmore campus.

5. The Beeson Center will sponsor and lead a program of computer communications, offering the library and media resources of Asbury Seminary to pastors through computer link-up. This will be in cooperation with the existing program of the library, expanding as resources and technology allow to make more and more of our resources accessible by computer link-up.
6. The Beeson Center will seek to network with pastors in order to identify pastoral needs to be addressed in the program, to provide resources to pastors, to identify potential participants in the various programs, and to provide ongoing opportunities for ministry for them.
7. The Beeson Center, in cooperation with the Pastoral Care Division of the Seminary, will sponsor the development of an Assessment Center for pastors and students. This center will offer personal testing and evaluation in order to help students understand their own gifts, values, and resources and develop personal vision and goals to guide them in their ministry.

Our Spirit

The Beeson Center for Biblical Preaching and Pastoral Leadership seeks to serve pastors and the church. We seek to form bridges between the academic world and the pastor, between the seminary and the church, between the gospel proclaimed and a culture in need of Christ.

The Center will be a focus for learning and personal growth. Excellence in ministry involves using the right tools for the right purpose. But, ministry begins with individuals who have surrendered their lives to service in the name of Christ. The church needs the Spirit of God unleashed through committed individuals who combine wisdom and skill in the execution of their ministry. We will seek to foster a marriage of mind and Spirit in the context of preaching and ministry.

We will not be a place where stock formulas are given. We will seek to grow a community where people bring practical needs and find wisdom, encouragement, and challenge.

We will listen to the world, respectfully and carefully. But, modern American culture will not ask all our questions, nor supply all the answers. We will seek to be a community that listens most attentively to God and God's word, and to respond in obedience.

EVALUATING A PURPOSE STATEMENT

The list below can be used as a guide to evaluate a statement of purpose. The goal is to devise a statement that really represents what the organization wants to be or should be to survive.

1. Broadness of scope and continuity of application: The statement should be broad enough to cover all significant areas of activity expected of the organization without a specific termination period indicated.
2. Functional commitment: The nature of the works, tasks, or activities to be performed must be defined in terms that will determine clearly the validity of the group or organization.
3. Resource commitment: The statement should include a commitment to cost-effective utilization of available resources.
4. Unique or distinctive nature of work: Every unit in an organization should make some unique or at least distinctive contribution. If there are two or more peer units in an organization with identical mission statements, the risk of duplicated effort is obvious.
5. Description of services to be offered.
6. Description of group or groups to be served.
7. Geographical area to be covered.

Sometimes it is useful to use a series of questions to evaluate a purpose statement after it is written. A "no" answer to one of the questions means the statement needs to be reworded to more clearly reflect the organization's basic reason for being. The following lists of questions may be useful.

1. Does it contain all important commitments?
2. Does it clearly state the function?
3. Is there a clear determination of relationships to the rest of the organization?
4. Is it distinct from the mission statements of other groups in the organization?

5. Is it short, to the point, and understandable?
6. Is it continuing in nature?
7. Does it state to whom the group is accountable?

Generally, a purpose statement can reflect whether the church wants to be local, regional, national, or international, the needs to be met, and so forth. The word "service" is often included in the mission statement of any organization.

The purpose statement needs to answer the question of why your church or ministry is needed in the first place. Plenty of other organizations exist. Discuss and know specifically what need you are meeting. For example, Victory Christian Center in Tulsa determined it was a local church with an international outreach. Morris Cerullo World Evangelism, based in San Diego, is truly an international ministry. Victory Christian Center and World Evangelism are quite different, but their primary reason for being is the same.

In an established denominational church, the focal purpose statement must reflect the support of the overall church statement of purpose. For example, a local Methodist church purpose statement should reflect the overall beliefs and doctrine of the United Methodist Church. John Wesley's own statement of the purpose of a Methodist Society is described in *The Nature, Design, and General Rules of the United Societies* (1743).

A company—united in order to pray together, to receive the word of exhortation, and to watch over one another in love, that they may help each other to work out their salvation.

Denominational organizations thus must make sure their purpose is aligned with the overall denomination's purpose. For example, when the pastor of one city's First United Methodist Church led his staff through this planning process, they all had to be constantly aware of the basic Methodist beliefs to be sure the purpose statement reflected those beliefs. This does not mean that the First United Methodist Church does not have the freedom of an unaligned or nondenominational church to have a vision and dream. It just means that the church had to be conscious of its roots to remain consistent.

SUMMARY

By verbalizing and putting in writing the vision God has given you for your church or ministry, you, in effect, state the unique reason God has brought your organization into existence. This provides the sense of direction and focus for what you do. What you do must be a function of who you are. The statement of purpose translates what God has divinely ordained into a mission for your church or ministry to fulfill.

PURPOSE STATEMENT WORKSHEET

This worksheet is provided to aid your church or ministry in starting the strategic planning process.

1. Write a statement for the following areas:
Congregational care statement: _____

_____

_____

_____

_____

Outreach and evangelism statement:_____

_____

_____

_____

Witness and mission work statement:_____

_____

_____

_____

2. Now evaluate the statement using the list of questions provided earlier.

3. Next submit it to others familiar with your organization to evaluate your statement of purpose and offer suggestions on improving the statement. In other words, does the statement say to others what you want it to say?

Chapter 4

Analysis and Assumptions

It is the glory of God to conceal a matter; to search out a matter is the glory of kings.

–Proverbs 25:2

In this chapter we discuss the need to analyze the situation confronting the church or ministry, and to identify any assumptions on which the strategic plan will be based. We will first discuss the need to assess the environment within which the ministry operates to understand the nature of external influences. Next, we will address the role of internal analysis of the situation within the church or ministry. It is critical that all attributes (whether strengths or weaknesses) of the organization be understood as well as features of its external environment (consisting of opportunities and threats) in order to establish appropriate assumptions on which to develop plans. Consequently, this step in strategic planning is critical to the success of the process.

EXTERNAL ANALYSIS

It is vital for a church or ministry to gauge the environment within which it operates. This should be standard practice for all organizations. It is important to realize that anything that can happen probably will, and that there is no truly accurate way to predict what the future will bring. The only way we can manage change is to constantly monitor the environment within which we operate. Examples for business might be the trends we see in gross national product, governmental control, regulation, the labor movement, interest rates, consumer preference, industry surveys, marketing research, Dow Jones stock averages, recent commodity prices, and so forth.

This environmental analysis stage is where we look at the past, identify trends, and, in effect, take the pulse of the environment in which the organization operates. Environmental analysis should not be confused with an assumption.

As an example, an environmental analysis for a television ministry might include the following elements: ("Cable Connections for Christ" 1985)

- In August 1984, cable penetration was estimated at 42.9 percent of American television households by the Nielsen service, with 36.1 million of the 83.3 million homes with television having cable. Arbitron's estimates show U.S. Cable penetration to stand at 41 percent, or 34.5 million households.
- Pat Robertson, president of Christian Broadcasting Network (CBN), has stated that 11 million subscribers who have access to CBN are watching it in a given week.
- Research by the American Resource Bureau indicates that the total audience for religious programs is about ten million people, or roughly 10 percent of the adult viewing public.
- There are currently more than 60 syndicated religious programs broadcast, and dozens more that do not qualify for syndicated status and measurement.
- Twenty-four-hour Christian satellite networks deliver programming to cable stations across the United States.
- Like so much of its work, the church may be learning that cable television must be a local ministry if it is to be evangelistically effective.
- Most of the mass media ministries are used for education and growth, reaching the already churched. But in local neighborhoods, cable television has proven to be an effective witness for converting the unsaved to Christ.
- Cable television is one of the best methods of extending the walls of the church and enlarging the outreach of its ministry into the local community.

- Television can be a tremendous public relations tool. Many churches today never have any influence in their community. Many are nonexistent as far as their community is concerned . . . they have no voice, influence, or even contact with those outside their fellowship.
- Ministry via cable television–when it is coupled with a local church–provides a nonthreatening medium through which viewers can participate.

ASSESSING OPPORTUNITIES AND THREATS

Opportunities and threats related to the external environment are analyzed to determine if any action (strategy) is needed to deal with them. For example, a large number of homeless people in a downtown area close to a church could provide an opportunity for ministry aimed at this group, and for a specific outreach program for this group. Alternatively, the church may decide that, even though the opportunity exists, they do not have the resources to begin ministry. Opportunities cannot be pursued if they are not recognized and analyzed.

The same is true for threats. A ministry that is not well financed and in heavy debt may risk losing a key leader due to death or illness or the "halo" effect of bad publicity of other ministries as a threat to the existence or at least the effectiveness of the ministry. Recognizing threats and analyzing the possible ramifications of events helps avoid many crises by developing contingency plans for dealing with such situations. Some have referred to this as "what if" and "what then" analysis. In other words, asking the questions "What if this happens?" and then "What do we do if this happens?" helps a church or ministry deal with major events which might be detrimental to the organization.

External analysis should evaluate at least seven factors (Migliore 1988, 74):

1. Economic trends in the locality, the geographic region, and the nation. Examples of these trends are changes in personal income, employment, land values, and industry location.

2. Demographic trends including shifts in age groups, education levels, numbers of widows and retired people, and shifts of population to different geographic areas.
3. Community issues of urban versus suburban development, growth or decline of commercial activities, and transportation facilities.
4. Changes in the services offered to people in the community. Who is offering the services? Are services primarily shifting into governmental hands or private sponsorship? How effective are these services in meeting the needs of the community?
5. Trends in competition for prime-time Sunday mornings and evenings and perhaps weekday evenings. What other things are going on that present competition for that time?
6. Church attendance trends in the community and region and reasons for changes in these trends. What activities in churches are proving to be the most popular at this time?
7. Changes in social values. What do people in the community view as important? Is churchgoing an important value? Evaluation in this area can involve issues such as the strength of family relationships, attitudes toward moral values, and so forth.

This stage in the planning process does not merely involve gathering data, getting it on paper, and forgetting about it. The environment must be constantly monitored.

INTERNAL ANALYSIS

At the organization level, another step in a thorough analysis is a full audit of the organization. A complete study of the church's emphasis on its ministries, management, policies, and procedures is needed. Also included in this environmental analysis is a study of the management system. A management questionnaire gives management information on the effectiveness of the management system and brings major problems to the surface. A method for auditing the planning system is needed. One way of doing this is through a questionnaire reviewing the planning environment, organizational structure, management philosophy and style, planning process, and other factors relating to the organization. The result is a thorough understanding of the planning system. The data collected in the audit can then be analyzed to determine strengths and weaknesses in the planning system. The most important are then included in the strengths-and-weaknesses part of the planning process.

It is useful to build a data base. The congregation or partner base should be one element studied. The more you know about the people being served, the better you can meet their needs. Many successful businesses, such as Wal-Mart, are continually doing research to learn more about their customers. A ministry should do the same thing. Information can be gathered on such factors as family size, marital status, age levels, where people work, people's needs, how long members have been in the congregation, whether people own or rent, and where they live. All of these are good questions to ask. For example, Victory Christian Center developed a profile of its congregation using modern marketing research techniques and found that 53 percent are under age 35, 48 percent have been attending Victory one year or less, 52 percent live within five miles of the church, 31 percent are single, 8 percent are single parents, and so forth. Several examples of questionnaires which could be modified for use in conducting an analysis of constituents are presented in Appendix E.

The Church and Community Survey Workbook, published by the Southern Baptist Convention Press, Nashville, Tennessee, does a good job of describing how to conduct meaningful surveys. The book contains sample questions and many fine ideas. It is a must for anyone involved in serious church or ministry planning.

ASSESSING STRENGTHS AND WEAKNESSES

After you have identified the purpose and considered the environment in which you operate, it is important to objectively assess the strengths and weaknesses of your church or ministry. In doing this, planners can learn from athletic coaches. They are constantly assessing the strengths and weaknesses of their team and the opponent, they try to maximize their strengths on game day, and improve on their weaknesses during practice. Organizations have certain strengths which make them uniquely suited to carry out their tasks.

Conversely, they have certain weaknesses which inhibit their abilities to fulfill their purposes. Like athletic coaches, managers who hope to accomplish their tasks need to carefully evaluate the strengths and weaknesses of the organization.

Among the things to evaluate are human, financial, facilities, equipment, and natural resources (Migliore 1988, 83-85):

1. financial resources of the church including operating funds, special funds, income, and expenditures
   - What has been our performance over the last five years in adhering to budget limits?
   - What is our ability to raise funds when needed?
2. equipment and space
   - Is it adequate for present needs and for planning future needs?
   - Is it in good operating condition?
   - Is it costly to maintain or operate?
3. the demographics of the congregation
   - How many people do we have in each age group?
   - What are the basic categories of jobs and income levels?
   - What percentage of the congregation consists of retired people or widows?
4. sociological profile of the church
   - Are we conservative or liberal?
   - Are we community minded?
   - Does our church collaborate with other community agencies and institutions?
   - As a church, what are our primary interests and social values?
5. power structure of the church
   - Who makes the decisions and by what process?
6. church organization and management
   - Quality of staffing, lay leadership, personnel policies, financial, and business management capabilities, organizational structure.
7. present programs
   - What are they?
   - Is the leadership in each program effective?

- How much interest and support from the congregation does each program have?

It is fairly easy to identify the strengths in each of these areas. When you attempt to define weaknesses, it becomes a little more painful. Often, organizations must engage outside consultants to be able to candidly pinpoint their limitations. But weaknesses and limitations must be recognized before you move on. All the evaluations listed in the environmental analysis can be separated into strengths and weaknesses.

Often church planning groups identify strengths first and write them on a blackboard. Through discussions, the group agrees on perhaps five major strengths. Then each person writes two or three weaknesses of the organization down on paper, which are copied onto the board to generate discussion. Only with a candid appraisal of strengths and weaknesses can realistic objectives be set.

MAKING ASSUMPTIONS

The next step is to make your major assumptions about spheres over which you have little or absolutely no control (e.g., the external environment). One good place to start is to extend some of the items studied in the external analysis.

Assumptions inherent in the field of church or ministry management might well include such statements as those listed below:

1. Television and radio programming costs will continue to skyrocket, especially during prime time.
2. Church-related capital will remain tax exempt, and contributions to church and ministry organizations will continue to be tax deductible.
3. Nursery care during the Sunday morning service will remain a priority item sought after by mothers of infants.
4. Providing a family service during the week will continue to (a) enhance church unity and (b) be an effective means to teach members on such issues as proper tithing practice.

A common thread is noted in church ministries that are growing and thriving under their founders. In such organizations plans have the basic assumption that these people remain in good health and continue as senior pastors. These founding pastors are important to the continued success of their ministries.

A list of certain assumptions that characterize the church/ministry should be developed. Assumptions are those thoughts and ideas that we take for granted about ourselves, God, and others. These assumptions are basic beginning points in the church's care, interest, and concern for people.

Below are some assumptions that fit the strategic planning model.

1. Quality leads to quantity. The quality of faith leads to greatness of faith. The quality of care for people leads to more people.
2. A commitment to excellence produces confidence in ministry and care. If I am committed to excellence in my personal life spiritually, emotionally, educationally, professionally, and socially, then people will have confidence in my interest in and care of them.
3. The Holy Spirit, along with the church, is able, willing, and free to break in and carry on His work in nonspectacular, nonmanipulative and surprising ways.
4. Each church is a new creation and should have differing forms of style and practices suited to that particular group.
5. You cannot manufacture the Holy Spirit's genuine working. You can only be in a position to see and enjoy it when it happens.

Assumptions must be directly related to action. Note the relationship between assumption and proposed action in the following example.

Assumption: Assume that a battleship fleet port will be located in the Lake Charles, Louisiana, area.

The plan for a church in the Lake Charles, Louisiana area is based in part on the external analysis that has thoroughly looked at what is going on in that area. In this case, you see that there is a chance for real economic change, new prosperity, people moving in, and so forth. Then you base your plan on an assumption. You either assume the port is in your area or you do not. How does this translate into action?

Action: Negotiate a land option.

That overgrown lot next to the church that has been an eyesore for years will go up in value in a hurry if the port is located in the area. Now is the time to negotiate an option to buy to cover a two-year period, not in five years when the need is great and the price is sky-high. The planner should also protect the church if the naval base goes somewhere else. With declining industry in the area, it is possible land values could go down.

The key is knowing what is going on and being alert to opportunities. Then develop a full plan based on a few assumptions. If an assumption changes, the plan changes.

The outline in Appendix B is a useful tool for internal and external analysis. Answering all the questions can be a good start in assessing the organization in several areas.

SUMMARY

This chapter emphasized the importance of coming to grips with the external and internal environments in which you must work to fulfill your mission. Minimizing weaknesses and capitalizing on strengths helps bolster the ability of an organization to operate in its external environment. Specifying the assumptions provides a basis for thoughtful consideration of the basic premises on which you operate. They should also cause you to ponder the "What if," "What then" scenarios that help avoid disruptions in the organization's operations through contingency planning.

ANALYSIS AND ASSUMPTIONS WORKSHEET

This worksheet will aid you in applying the concepts discussed in this chapter to your church or ministry.

1. List key environmental factors for your plan

NATIONAL:
  1. _____
  2. _____
  3. _____
  4. _____
  5. _____

REGIONAL:
  1. _____
  2. _____
  3. _____
  4. _____
  5. _____

LOCAL:
  1. _____
  2. _____
  3. _____
  4. _____
  5. _____

2. List the assumptions on which your plan is based

  1. _____
  2. _____
  3. _____
  4. _____
  5. _____

Chapter 5

Establishing Objectives

I press on toward the goal to win the prize for which God has called me heavenward in Christ Jesus.

–Phil. 3:14

In this chapter we discuss establishing objectives, the third step in the strategic planning process. After the purpose or mission of the church or ministry has been defined, internal and external analysis completed, and assumptions made, then–and only then–can objectives be considered.

One writer has said, "You cannot achieve goals if you do not have any. Sometimes this idea is so simple that many people overlook it. In order to accomplish anything, we have to first purpose in our hearts to do it. We have to make up our minds. If we do not, we just waste our time and energy and find ourselves going around in circles, looking back at the past and wondering where it went" (Roberts 1977, 10, 11).

NATURE AND ROLE OF OBJECTIVES

The words key results, goals, and targets are often used synonymously when talking about long- and short-term objectives. Whatever the term used, the idea is to focus on a specific set of target activities and outcomes to be accomplished. Think of the analogy of the archer used earlier. A pastor wants his whole church aimed at the same target just as an archer wants his arrow aimed at the bull's-eye. People get confused and disorganized if they do not know where they are going. The success or failure of a nonprofit organization is based on its ability to set goals, as well as on tools with which to measure progress.

There are at least six reasons why nonprofit organizations (such as churches and ministries) fail to set clearcut objectives.

1. Many nonprofit managers fear accountability.
2. Many projects continue even when they no longer serve an organization's goals.
3. Nonprofits normally undertake any activity for which money is available.
4. Some nonprofit managers fear hard-nosed evaluation may undermine humanitarian instincts.
5. Nonprofit managers must spend a great deal of time on activities that do not further their goals (meeting with donors, fund raising, explaining programs, and so forth).
6. Nonprofits have no financial report cards to tell them how they are doing. (Harvey and Sander 1987)

As objectives are established in the organization, some of these reasons may not be applicable. However, most of this list could be applied in any type of organizational setting.

Objectives are clear, concise written statements outlining what is to be accomplished in key areas in a certain time period, in objectively measurable terms. Objectives can be classified as routine, problem solving, innovative, team, personal, and budget performance. Drucker states that "objectives are not fate; they are direction. They are not commands, but they are commitments. They do not determine the future, but they are the means by which the resources and energies of the operation can be mobilized for the making of the future" (1954, 102). Objectives can be set at upper organizational levels in areas such as growth, finances, physical resources, staff development and attitudes. They are also needed in sub-units, departments, or divisions of an organization. Most important, all organizational objectives must be consistent. Thus, a department's objectives should lead to accomplishing the overall organization's goals.

Objectives serve two fundamental purposes. First, they serve as a road map. Objectives are the results desired upon completion of the planning period. In the absence of objectives, no sense of direction can be attained in decision making. In planning, objectives answer one of the basic questions posed in the planning process: Where do we want to go? These objectives become the focal point for strategy decisions.

Another basic purpose served by objectives is in the evaluation of performance. The objectives in the strategic plan become the yardsticks used to evaluate performance. It is impossible to evaluate performance without some standard with which results can be compared. The objectives become the standards for evaluating performance because they are the statement of results desired by the planner.

Objectives are often considered the neglected area of management because in many situations there is a failure to set objectives, or the objectives which are set forth are unsound and therefore lose much of their effectiveness. In fact, a fairly recent approach to management, called management by objectives (MBO), has emphasized the need for setting objectives as a basic managerial process.

ALTERNATIVES TO MANAGING BY OBJECTIVES

One way to be convinced of the usefulness and power of managing by objectives is to consider some of the alternatives. (Thompson and Strickland 1986, 52)

1. *Managing By Extrapolation (MBE).* This approach relies on the principle "If it ain't broke, don't fix it." The basic idea is to keep on doing about the same things in about the same ways because what you are doing (1) works well enough and (2) has gotten you this far. The basic assumption is that, for whatever reason, "your act is together," so why worry?; the future will take care of itself and things will work out all right.

2. *Managing By Crisis (MBC).* This approach to administration is based upon the concept that the strength of any really good manager is solving problems. Since there are plenty of crises around–enough to keep everyone occupied–managers ought to focus their time and energy on solving the most pressing problems of today. MBC is, essentially, reactive rather than proactive, and the events that occur dictate management decisions.

3. *Managing By Subjectives (MBS).* The MBS approach occurs when no organization-wide consensus or clear-cut directives exist on which way to head and what to do. Each manager

translates this to mean do your best to accomplish what you think should be done. This is a "do your own thing the best way you know how" approach. This is also referred to as "the mystery approach." Managers are left on their own with no clear direction ever articulated by senior management.

4. *Managing By Hope (MBH).* In this approach, decisions are predicated on the hope that they will work out and that good times are just around the corner. It is based on the belief that if you try hard enough and long enough, then things are bound to get better. Poor performance is attributed to unexpected events and the fact that decisions always have uncertainties and surprises. Much time is therefore spent hoping and wishing things will get better.

All four of these approaches represent "muddling through." Absent is any effort to calculate what is needed to influence where an organization is headed and what its activities should be to reach specific objectives. In contrast, managing by objectives is much more likely to achieve targeted results and have a sense of direction.

CHARACTERISTICS OF GOOD OBJECTIVES

For objectives to serve as a means of providing direction and as a standard for evaluation, they must possess certain characteristics. The more of these attributes possessed by a given objective, the more likely it will achieve its basic purpose. Sound objectives should have the following characteristics:

1. *Objectives should be clear and concise.* There should not be any room for misunderstanding what results are sought in a given objective. The use of long statements with words or phrases which may be defined or interpreted in different ways by different people should be avoided.

2. *Objectives should be in written form.* This helps to provide effective communication and to discourage the altering of unwritten objectives over time. Everyone realizes that oral statements can be unintentionally altered as they are communicated. Written statements avoid this problem and permit ease

of communication. A second problem with unwritten objectives is that they tend to be altered to fit current circumstances.

3. *Objectives should name specific results in key areas.* The key areas in which objectives are needed will be identified later in this chapter. Specific desired results, such as "100,000 dollars in annual contributions" rather than a "high level of contributions" or "an acceptable level of contributions," should be used to avoid doubt about what result is sought.

4. *Objectives should be stated for a specific time period.* For example, objectives that are set for a short-run, more immediate time period such as six months to one year must be accomplished as a prerequisite to longer-run objectives. The time period specified becomes a deadline for producing results and also sets up the final evaluation of the success of a strategy.

5. *Objectives should be stated in measurable terms.* Concepts which defy precise definition and qualification should be avoided. "Goodwill" is an example of a concept which is important, but which in itself is difficult to define and measure. If a planner decides that goodwill is a concept which must be measured, a substitute measure or measures will have to be used. An objective related to goodwill which would be capable of quantification might be stated as follows: "To have at least 85 percent of our constituents rate our church as the best church in the area in our annual survey." Phrases such as "high attendance" not only are not clear or specific, but cannot be measured. Does high mean first, second, or third in attendance? Is it a specific number, or a percent? If the statement is quantified as "Increase attendance by 10 percent by December 1," it can be objectively measured. The accomplishment or failure of such a stated objective can be readily evaluated.

6. *Objectives must be consistent with overall organizational objectives and purpose.* This idea has been previously stated, but must be continually reemphasized because of the need for organizational unity.

7. *Objectives should be attainable, but of sufficient challenge to stimulate effort.* Two problems can be avoided if this characteristic is achieved. One is the avoidance of frustration produced by objectives which cannot be attained, or which cannot

be attained within the specified time period. If an organization already has an unusually large attendance, the desirability and likelihood of substantial increases in attendance are doubtful. The other problem is setting objectives which are so easy to attain that only minimum effort is needed. This results in an unrealistic performance evaluation and does not maximize the contribution of a given strategic plan.

One approach to writing objectives which contain these characteristics is to apply a set of criteria to each statement to increase the probability of good objectives. One such list follows.

1. *Relevance.* Are the objectives related to and supportive of the basic purpose of the organization?
2. *Practicality.* Do the objectives take into consideration obvious constraints?
3. *Challenge.* Do the objectives provide a challenge?
4. *Measurability.* Are the objectives capable of some form of quantification, if only on an order-of-magnitude basis?
5. *Schedule.* Are the objectives so constituted that they can be time phased and monitored at interim points to ensure progress toward their attainment?
6. *Balance.* Do the objectives provide for a proportional emphasis on all activities and keep the strengths and weaknesses of the organization in proper balance?

Objectives that meet such criteria are much more likely to serve their intended purpose. The resulting statements can then serve as the directing force in the development of strategy. Consider the following examples of poorly stated objectives:

Poor: Our objective is to maximize attendance.

How much is "maximum"? The statement is not subject to measurement. What criterion or yardstick will be used to determine if and when actual attendance is equal to the maximum? No deadline is specified.

Better: Our objective is to achieve an attendance target for worship services in three years averaging 1000 per week.

Poor: Our objective is to increase contributions.

How much? A one-dollar increase will meet that objective, but is that really the desired target?
Better: Our objective this calendar year is to increase contributions from 300,000 to 350,000 dollars.

Poor: Our objective is to boost advertising expenditures by 15 percent.

Advertising is an activity, not a result. The advertising objective should be stated in terms of what result the extra advertising is intended to produce.
Better: Our objective is to boost our viewing audience from 8 percent to 10 percent in the next five years with the help of a 15 percent increase in advertising expenditures.

Poor: Our objective is to be the best church in our area.

Not specific enough; what measures of "best" are to be used? Attendance? Contributions? New programs started? Services offered? Number of converts?
Better: We will strive to become the number-one church in the metropolitan area in terms of new converts baptized within five years.

Keep the following suggestions in mind when writing objectives (Hale 1984, 5-13):

1. Objectives should start with the word "to" followed by an action verb, since the achievement of an objective must come as a result of specific action;
2. Objectives should specify a single major result to be accomplished so the group will know precisely when the objective has been achieved;
3. An objective should have a target date for accomplishment;
4. The objective should relate directly to the mission statement of the group or individual. A parish council liturgy committee should not write an objective outside the scope of its own mission statement or one that pertains more to the mission statement of the parish council. This may seem obvious, but groups often commit themselves to projects for which they have neither responsibility nor authority;
5. The objective must be understandable to those who will be working to achieve the specified results;

6. The objective must be possible to achieve;
7. The objective should be consistent with parish and diocesan policies and practices.

TYPES OF OBJECTIVES INCLUDED IN A STRATEGIC PLAN

Five-year objectives can be set in areas such as attendance, programs offered, missionary support, building programs, and so forth. For example, "Key Result Areas" for setting objectives could include:

1. level of membership
2. level and sources of funds
3. neighborhood acceptance
4. youth participation
5. quantity of programs
6. quality of programs
7. leadership effectiveness
8. quantity and quality of services (McConkey 1978, 21)

Strategic plans for churches and ministries usually contain at least three types of objectives: attendance (and/or listening/viewing), contributions, and constituents. Short-term objectives are stated for the operating period only, normally one year, whereas long-term objectives usually span five to 20 years.

Attendance Objectives

Attendance or audience objectives relate to an organization's impact on an area, and are a basic measure of the level of activity for a program or service. Attendance objectives are closely tied to scheduling of services, budgeting, and so on.

Many people have difficulty with the emphasis on numbers and certainly if growing larger for the sake of "being big" is our motive, it is completely out of line with Biblical teachings. God deals with individuals; individuals make commitments, help others, serve, etc. However, a different perspective can also be used for the emphasis on numbers.

The pastor of a newly formed church in a small town in Arkansas made a couple of insightful statements about numbers. The church meets at a Days Inn because it has no building. The pastor's brother is associate pastor and music director and both their wives play instruments and/or sing in the services. Sunday school for youth and children is held in motel rooms. After only four months of existence the church already had had attendance in excess of 100 several times with a theme of "Everyone Bring One." The pastor explained the theme by stating that people have to be reached; an empty chair has never been saved, made a commitment, helped others, or asked for prayer. He went on to say that if the church is spreading the Gospel and meeting people's needs, it will grow; and if it is not it should not be here.

Attendance objectives may be stated numerically or as a percent of the total number. If the objectives are stated in percents, they also need to be converted to numbers for budgeting and estimating the audience size. Examples of attendance objectives are given in Exhibit 5-1. The way objectives are stated must reflect what the organization can realistically expect to attain under a given plan. Also, the steps of setting objectives and developing strategy in preparing a marketing plan should be viewed as interactive. In setting objectives, we first state them in terms of what we want to accomplish, but as we develop the strategy we may discover that we cannot afford what we want. The available resources committed to a given program or service may not be sufficient to achieve a stated objective; and if the planning process is resource-controlled, the objectives must be altered. It must be remembered that objectives are not fate, but they are direction. They are not commands, but they become commitments. As a planner, you must not fall into the trap of thinking that once objectives are set they cannot be altered.

Each of the objectives in Exhibit 5-1 is clear, concise, quantifiable, and stated within a given time period. Only objective 2 requires external data to evaluate whether it was accomplished. Total audience size would be required to compute the percentage.

Contribution Objectives

Contributions are a vital part of any church or ministry. While they are never ends in themselves, they are the enabling resources that are needed by an organization. However, there is a more practical reason for including a specific statement about contributions: It forces the planner to estimate the resources needed to underwrite specific programs and services. A statement of whether resources will be available cannot be made without at least some analysis of the cost of providing services for activities which must break even. For new programs, the expenditures and contributions associated with the program should have been analyzed before introduction. For existing programs, contributions can be analyzed to project continued levels of support. This information, combined with estimates of expenses involved in implementing the marketing strategy, provides a basis for statements of objectives about contributions.

Sample statements are shown in Exhibit 5-2 as illustrations of contribution objectives. Again, nebulous statements such as "acceptable contribution levels" or "reasonable contributions" should be avoided because of the possible variations in definition and the lack of quantifiability. The objective of a percentage increase in contributions is the only one requiring additional information for its evaluation. The amount of the total previous contribution would be required to determine whether this objective has been reached.

Keep in mind that the interactive processes of setting objectives and developing strategies must be used to set objectives that are realistic. The costs of many aspects of strategy cannot be estimated until a written statement of strategy is developed. If the strategy calls for a new program, for example, that strategy must be spelled out in detail before costs can be estimated.

EXHIBIT 5-1
Examples of Attendance-Oriented Objectives

1. Achieve average attendance of 500 for Sunday School within three years.
2. Have 50 percent of the potential TV audience view our annual Christmas special this year.

Constituent Objectives

Constituent objectives may seem unusual to some, but their inclusion should be obvious. They serve as enabling objectives in attendance and contributions, and also represent specific statements of constituent behaviors and/or attitudes an organization would want members to have toward its programs and services.

Constituent objectives are especially important in providing direction to the development of the strategy section of the plan. As shown in Exhibit 5-3, they specify results desired of constituents in terms of behaviors and attitudes, and should have the same characteristics as other objectives. They must be stated in objectively measurable terms and should be evaluated in relation to their accomplishment as a part of the monitoring and control system used in the plan.

USING ENVIRONMENTAL ANALYSIS DATA TO SET OBJECTIVES

The objectives of a given plan are based on the data provided in the analysis discussed earlier. In other words, good objectives are based on a careful analysis of the external and internal environment of the church or ministry. A specific example of how data are used in setting objectives may help in understanding this point.

A large church in a city of approximately 400,000 people had a very low and declining number of youth age 13 to 18. The church had a youth facility capable of handling up to 300 young people. The environmental factors were, for the most part, favorable, and the total youth population had a healthy growth rate.

EXHIBIT 5-2
Examples of Contribution Objectives

1. Produce net contributions of 180,000 dollars by year five.
2. Generate a 20 percent increase in contributions within five years.
3. Produce a contribution of 85,000 dollars for the summer youth camp within three years.

The analysis identified three market segments for youth services, one of which was for after-school activities. This was a unique segment with special needs in terms of transportation, types of services and facilities desired, and timing of the events.

The number of youth was found in public records available through the school system, and the number interested in after-school programs was estimated through a telephone survey of a sample of 50 youths. The resulting analysis is shown in Exhibit 5-4.

Objectives derived through such a process represent the realities of the area and also the church's willingness and ability to commit itself to such objectives. This example should also reemphasize the logic in the strategic planning format. The analysis precedes the setting of objectives, because realistic objectives must be derived from the results of the analysis.

EXHIBIT 5-3
Examples of Constituent Objectives

1. Create at least 20 percent participation in our new missions program within a three year period.
2. Have at least 80 percent of our members rate the quality of our programs as "very good" in our annual survey of members.

EXHIBIT 5-4
Potential for After-School Youth Program

1. Population in metropolitan area = 400,000
2. Number of youth in metropolitan area (13-18 years old) = 37,200
3. Number of youth within church's primary market area = 3,000
4. Percent of youth in telephone survey who say they are interested in after-school programs at church = 10 percent (i.e., five out of 50 called)
5. Total number of youth who represent a viable target = 300 (i.e., 3,000 x .10)
6. Objective: Attract an average of 300 youths per week within three years.

PERFORMANCE CONTRACTS

Objectives can become the basis of a performance contract for staff members. As an example, note how the objectives for an associate pastor can become a performance contract through the following process:

1. properly written objectives submitted to the pastor
2. items discussed and negotiated with the pastor
3. objectives resubmitted to the pastor
4. list approved by both parties (and perhaps the pastor/parish relations committee)
5. in some organizations, both parties sign an objectives sheet

PERIODIC REVIEW

One practical, easy way to record, communicate, measure, and update objectives is through a "Performance Plan Book" or "Management Plan Book." All objectives for the organization should be in this book. Objectives are to be reviewed each quarter and updated. Shown below are examples of how objectives can be listed, tracked, and presented for review. This process greatly reduces paperwork and provides a convenient method for review. Examples are of overall church objectives that encourage a look into the future. They take into account key result areas and suggestions by more than 50 pastors and scholars.

OVERALL CHURCH OBJECTIVES, 1996-1998

	1996	1997	1998
STAFF			
Pastor			
Assistants			

	1996	1997	1998

ATTENDANCE
   First services
   Second services
   Sunday School
   Sunday night
   Wednesday night
   Revivals
   Training seminars

MEMBERSHIP

BUILDINGS
   Build a new church
   Facilities improvement
   Added equipment

MISSIONS OUTREACH
   Contribution (to central fund)
   Other mission trips
   Annual Mexico trips
   Calling (lay) people involved
   Number of calls
      1. Evangelism
      2. Hospital
      3. Post-hospital
      4. Inactive
      5. Home department
      6. Nursing homes

FACILITIES
   Annual safety check
   Sound system
   Heating and cooling
   Burglar alarms
   Lighting
   Parking

	1996	1997	1998

PROGRAMS
Children
Youth
Young adults, college age
Men, women, senior citizens
Divorce recovery
Widowed
Alcoholic recovery
Marriage enrichment
Caring calling
Family life
Political and social action
Lay ministry training

PEOPLE/TRAINING MORALE
House training per staff
Retreat days for minister
Retreat days for laity
Retreats
Yearly attitude survey
Small groups: types, number
Counseling participants
Ministerial
Lay
Alcoholics, drug abusers
Divorcees/widows

PUBLIC RESPONSIBILITY
Use facilities for civic club lunches
Sponsor Boy Scout and Girl Scout troop
Social service
Relief
Talking books
Prison ministry
Meals-on-wheels

<u>1996</u>   <u>1997</u>   <u>1998</u>

Personal growth
1. Initiate daily devotions
2. Attend growth seminars

FINANCIAL
Average collections (per service)
Budget
Current ratio
New tithers
New pledgers
Stewardship of persons
New persons accepting responsibility
New lay ministers
New candidates for ordained ministry
Fixed asset turnover/collections/net fixed assets
Total asset turnover/collections/total assets
Debt ratio/total debt/total assets
Debt/total collections
Times interest earned/collections/interest

REVIEW SHEET
MANAGEMENT PLAN, 1996

I. Routine
Set aside 5,000 dollars for
overseas missions
programs throughout
every month of 1996   On target

II. Problem Solving
Develop an efficient
transportation routing
schedule to be followed
by the bus outreach
captains by March 31, 1996   Met 90 percent

III. Innovative
     Devise a better layout for
     member parking during
     February 1996   Done

IV. Personal
    Read the book *MBO:*
    Blue Collar to Top
    Executive, attend
    Communication Course,
    Fall of 1996

V. Budget Performance
   Operate within the
   50,000 dollar church budget
   throughout fiscal 1996   On target

CHURCH ADMINISTRATOR'S OBJECTIVES, 1996

 I. Routine
    1. Make at least one hospital visit per week
    2. Exercise four times per week
    3. Review each committee chair's objectives and accomplish-
       ments by January 5, May 5, and August 5
    4. Attend the annual state pastors' meeting

II. Problem-Solving
    1. Develop a project for the 11- to 14-year-old youth to make
       a contribution to the community
    2. Develop youth minister internship plan with local pastors
       by January 31
    3. Develop a set of criteria and measurable objectives for the
       Sunday school retreat
    4. Hold a one-day symposium on the spititual and mental
       health of young people; prepare summary minutes and
       recommendations for improvement within three years

III. Innovative
  1. Devise a better system of screening prospective church employees
  2. Develop a method or methods to give all committee chairs feedback on their budget performance. At least one method to be implemented by May 1, and another method implemented by June 1, 1998

IV. Personal
  1. Improve my understanding of the Bible (I will read three pages per day and attend at least one Bible-study group.)
  2. Do not miss one Sunday service

V. Team
  1. Work with the organist on revision and update of hymnbook to be introduced in July
  2. Meet with the pastor each Wednesday to coordinate the music with the sermon

VI. Budget
  1. Operate within the 100,000 dollar yearly budget
  2. Retire 10 percent of the debt on the church building

SUMMARY

Setting objectives is another major part of the strategic planning process. The necessity for objectives as well as their characteristics was presented here to lay the groundwork for identifying basic types of objectives, such as attendance, contributions, and constituents. The objectives provided as examples in this chapter can be used both as a source of direction and to evaluate the strategies developed in the plan.

OBJECTIVES WORKSHEET

This worksheet will aid you in applying the concepts discussed in this chapter to your church or ministry.

Answer These Questions First

1. What do your objectives need to relate to–attendance, contributions, constituents or all three? What about other key result areas? _____

_____

2. What needs to happen for your program to be successful? In other words, how many people need to attend/watch, join, contribute, volunteer, etc.? _____

_____

3. When do you want this to happen? By what specific date?

_____

_____

Now Write Your Objectives

Use the information in your answers to these three questions to write statements of your objectives.

Objective 1: _____

_____

_____

_____

Objective 2: _____

_____

_____

_____

Objective 3: _____

_____

_____

_____

Now test each statement using the criteria given in this chapter. Is each statement relevant to the basic purpose of your organization? Is each statement practical? Does each statement provide a challenge? Is each statement stated in objectively measurable terms? Do you have a specific date for completion? Does each statement contribute to a balance of activities in line with your church's strengths and weaknesses?

Chapter 6

Developing Strategy
and Operational Plans

May he give you the desire of your heart and make all your
plans succeed.

—Proverbs 20:4

After developing a set of objectives for the time period covered
by the strategic plan, you must formulate the strategy needed to
accomplish those objectives. You must first design an overall strategy. Then you must plan the operating details of that strategy, as it
relates to providing ministry services, promotion, determining location, and enlisting contributions, to guide the church's efforts. In
this chapter we introduce the concept of strategy and describe strategy elements and approaches to strategy development.

STRATEGY CONCEPTS

The word "strategy" has been used in a number of ways over the
years, especially in the context of business. Often, it is confused
with the terms "objectives," "policies," "procedures," "strategies," and "tactics." *Strategy* may be defined as the course of
action taken by an organization to achieve its objectives. It is the
catalyst or dynamic element of managing which enables a company
to accomplish its objectives.

Strategy development is both a science and an art and is a product of both logic and creativity. The scientific aspect deals with

assembling and allocating the resources necessary to achieve an organization's objectives with emphasis on opportunities, costs, and time. The art of strategy is mainly concerned with the utilization of resources, including motivation of the people, sensitivity to the environment, and ability to adapt to changing conditions.

ALTERNATE STRATEGIES

The alternate strategies considered by management are the alternate courses of action evaluated by management before committing to a specific course of action outlined in the strategic plan. Thus, strategy is the link between objectives and results.

There are two basic strategies a church or ministry can use to accomplish its objectives: a differentiated strategy and focus strategy. The chosen strategy must of course be an outgrowth of the organization's basic purpose.

Differentiated Strategy

A differentiated strategy is a strategy that entails developing services that are aimed at meeting a broad spectrum of needs. It is the strategy used by most churches that develop a whole gamut of programs. Research has shown that this is the best strategy for new churches in terms of generating increases in membership.

First Baptist Church of West Monroe, Louisiana uses this strategy. The church offers a wide variety of ministry programs.

Preschool and Children's Ministry

The areas of ministry involved are: (1) Christian education, through Sunday morning study; (2) special education, providing Bible-learning activities for mentally handicapped children and youth; and (3) vacation Bible school, provided each summer.

Youth Ministry (7th through 12th grades, or Junior High and High School)

The areas of ministry involved are: (1) Christian education through Sunday morning Bible study; (2) discipleship through Church Training each Sunday night and Disciple Now, a special weekend emphasis each year; and (3) special activities such as Agape House which is open on weekends for youth fellowship, witness training, snow skiing, summer camp, fall recreates, fellowships, banquets, recreational activities, special bible studies, and music.

Single Adult Ministry (includes never married, divorced, or widowed)

The areas of ministry involved are: (1) Christian education through Sunday morning Bible Study, and Sunday evening services; and (2) social activities including fellowship times at church and in homes, trips, special entertainment, retreats, and conferences.

Music Ministry

The areas of ministry involved are: choirs, vocal ensembles, and bell choirs spanning preschool, children, junior and senior high, and adults.

Recreation Ministry

The areas of ministry involving all age groups are: (1) sports, including teams and individuals, instructional classes, and church-wide tournaments; (2) Christian outdoor experiences, including group retreats, day and mission camps, youth camps, and other outdoor activities; and (3) crafts and continuing education classes.

Outreach ministry

The areas of ministry involved are: (1) venture revivals, in area churches by lay members; (2) special projects in missions, such as construction or renovation of mission churches or facilities; (3) missionary home, for Baptist missionaries home on furlough; and (4) visitation on a regular schedule.

By using a differentiated strategy, First Baptist Church thus targets a broad segment of markets ranging across preschool, children, youth, singles, families, adults, senior citizens, handicapped, etc.

Focus Strategy

A focus strategy is more likely to be used by a ministry because it involves concentrating on the needs of a specific group or on a specific type of ministry. Missions to Mexico, headquartered in Pharr, Texas, uses this strategy. Brother Edgar Stone has devoted his life's ministry to taking the Gospel to areas where there is no current work by any other Christian group. He has basically created a ministry that involves bringing in converts who feel a call to be pastors and putting them through a two-year educational program similar to seminary training. He then encourages these new pastors to return to their villages and he helps them to start a new church by paying up to one half of the construction cost. This has resulted in the construction of over 150 churches in Mexico over the last 30 years.

While Missions to Mexico may occasionally be involved in other forms of ministry, such as summer youth camps for the youth of the churches established through the ministry, its main thrust is equipping pastors and building new churches.

The main advantages of this strategy are: (1) It capitalizes on the distinctive competencies of the people involved; and (2) It concentrates on doing one thing well. These advantages can also create a knowledge base of how to carry out certain types of ministry as well as improved efficiency in performing the ministry.

FACTORS INFLUENCING THE STRATEGY SELECTED

At least four factors influence the choice of a strategy selected by the firm: the organization's resources, the distinctive competencies of leaders and members, stage in the organization's life cycle, and strategies used by other organizations. There is no one best strategy which will always prove successful. Instead, the strategy that is chosen must be the one that is best for the church or ministry, given the nature of these four factors. Resources, for example, may limit the organization to a focus strategy. The organization may even be an innovator in terms of ideas but not have the financial, communication, or personnel resources to offer other services.

As was emphasized in Chapter 2, the organization strategy must be derived from the organizational purpose and objectives. If the organizational purpose is focused on serving needs of diverse groups then the strategy used must be one that is compatible. In other words, what an organization *does* must be a function of what it *is*.

The distinctive competencies of the organization have a direct bearing on the strategy selected. Distinctive skills and experience in missions, for example, can influence strategy choice. These distinctive competencies are the basis of doing things well.

The organization's life-cycle stage is an additional factor influencing strategy selection. For example, an organization may begin with a focus strategy but add programs over time which serves more varied needs. Repositioning the organization through introducing new programs or serving new markets would be a pivotal point of the strategy.

The strategy selected must be given sufficient time to be implemented and affect groups served, but an obviously ineffective strategy should be changed. This concept should be understood without mention, but the resistance to change in many organizations is a common phenomenon.

OPERATIONAL PLANS

After all the steps have been taken and a strategy has been developed to meet your objectives and goals, it is time to create an operational or action plan. The operational plan is the "action" or "doing" stage. Here you hire, fire, build, advertise, and so on. How many times has a group of people planned something, become enthusiastic about it, and then nothing happened? This is usually because group leaders did not complete an operational or action plan to implement their strategy.

Operational plans must be developed in all the areas that are used to support the overall strategy. These include production, communication, finance, and staffing. Each of these more detailed plans is designed to spell out what needs to happen in a given area to implement the strategic plan.

The production plan identifies exactly what services will be provided to a specific group and the exact nature of those services. Will it be preaching, teaching, music, worship, or a combination of these activities? If a church is trying to launch mission work in an urban area of low income people, the work could take many forms. It could be a "satellite" church, a literacy program, or it could concentrate on housing and feeding the homeless. These, of course, are completely different types of activities and must be carefully planned.

The communication plan is used to communicate the nature of the program, location, and time to the intended audience and also to the rest of the church. This plan also needs to be well thought out and carefully analyzed to avoid a lack of communication or miscommunication.

For example, Christ Is The Answer, located in El Paso, Texas, in developing their operational plans, needed a communication strategy to provide information to people about their purpose and programs. The communication strategy involved three key elements: informing, persuading, and reminding.

1. *Informing*–This involves providing information to individuals and groups about the organizations. Specific elements of this plan call for:
   a. use of video cassette presentations
   b. newsletters, pamphlets, and prayer guides
   c. personal speaking appearances by ministry leaders
   d. hosting luncheons/dinners sponsored by supporters
   e. on-site visits by individuals/groups to headquarters or ministry centers
2. *Persuading*–This involves presenting the gospel message contained in the Great Commission as well as the principles from the apostle Paul's writings about the support he received while involved in mission work.
   a. Prepare application forms with which partners may request additional information or may apply as a team member.
   b. Provide opportunities for support by individuals through prayers and specific offerings for teams, supplies, and so forth.

3. *Reminding*–This aspect of the strategy is to continue to provide information to people already familiar with the ministry so they will be constantly reminded of the work and needs of the ministry.
   a. Send letters/newsletters and other materials regularly.
   b. Provide opportunities for team members to write supporters and future team members on a periodic basis.
   c. Develop a complete file of individuals and organizations by name for future mailings.

In the staffing plan you must identify who will carry out the activities involved. Will it be church/ministry staff or volunteers? If paid staff are to be used, will they be full-time or part-time? Of course, if volunteers are to be used, they must be recruited, trained and supervised. Since most churches must rely on the laity to carry out plans, it may be necessary to develop a recruitment plan just to staff the activity.

Finances must also be planned. This is usually done in the form of a financial budget. The budget is the means to execute the plan. If the financial means to support the plan are not available you must adjust the objectives. There is a constant interplay between the budget and the plan. Many people do not understand the budgeting process. The budget is a tool. Too often, however, the budget becomes the "tail wagging the dog." "We budgeted it so we had better spend it," or "We had better add a little to this year's budget" are statements that reflect this misunderstanding. Budget money must be tied directly to performance, and performance is measured against objectives. Key results and objectives in a church and ministry are prioritized, and then money and resources are allocated.

An example of this interplay came out of a meeting at a large church. Most of their resources for the next two years would have to go into finishing current building programs. Only enough money was available to maintain the status quo of the church school even though they wanted to expand it. That does not mean the school is not important–it is–but the timing for expansion and growth for the school cannot come until the other projects are completed.

The action plan for a large church with many different types of programs and ministries is depicted in Exhibit 6-1 and 6-2. The operational or action plan in this example is related directly to the strategy to be used and the objectives to be accomplished in a step-by-step fashion. This forces the planner to align objectives, strategies, and action plans.

Notice that the Action Plan format takes one objective out of the five-year strategic plan and isolates it for further study and analysis. In this case it shows the targets at which this church is aiming with its Home Groups and Children's Ministry. You never go into action until the target is clear and understood by everyone. It is important that all those who execute these plans be in on the planning and be aware of what is going on. That is the key to enthusiasm and support by the people. With targets/objectives/goals in mind, the

---

EXHIBIT 6-1
Action Plan: Home Groups

OBJECTIVE:
To have 150 home groups in the next five years (1994-1998).
    1994: 30 home groups
    1995: 45 home groups
    1996: 62 home groups
    1997: 95 home groups
    1998: 150 home groups

STRATEGIES:
    A. We plan to increase year by year as the total congregation grows so that we will be able to accommodate one-third to one-half of the congregation.
    B. We plan to add one home group pastor for every 50 home groups.

ACTION PLAN	PERSON RESPONSIBLE	START DATE	DATE COMPLETED

Pastor Brooks is training several hand-picked couples as future home-group leaders. Each present home-group leader is in the process of training an assistant leader. Each existing home group, plus all new home groups are to set a goal to split and become two groups each year. They are to begin training an assistant within their new home group.

```
┌─────────────────────────────────────────────────────────────┐
│                         EXHIBIT 6-2                           │
│                 Action Plan: Children's Ministry              │
├─────────────────────────────────────────────────────────────┤
```

OBJECTIVE:
To have 500 children attending full children's church services during each of
two adult morning services:
    1994-- 300
    1995-- 350
    1996-- 400
    1997-- 450
    1998-- 500

STRATEGIES:
  A. Develop complete teacher-recruitment training program
  B. Develop neighborhood outreach ministry for children
  C. Develop teacher training program
  D. Develop puppet ministry
  E. Hire full-time children's pastor

ACTION PLAN	PERSON RESPONSIBLE	START DATE	DATE COMPLETED
Hire part-time pastor			
Establish teacher training course and teacher recruitment strategy.			
Begin Saturday advertising campaign in community.			
Conduct four picnic-type outings a year to attract local children. Hire full-time children's pastor.			
Puppet ministry in two services.			
Update training services.			

various strategies are agreed upon. They are listed immediately under the objectives. Next, all the actions that must take place are listed. Also note that at the top of each section is a row to write who is in charge, date started, and date completed. This document becomes not only a guide to action but a timeline for starting and completing plans.

The person or persons responsible and the expected date of completion must be agreed upon. Every person involved gets a copy of the plan with his/her areas of responsibility marked. Now one person can coordinate a multitude of projects and programs, because there is a clear record of what is to be done. As each action or task is completed, the person responsible sends in a completion report. With this approach, the coordinator knows what is going on all the time.

The action plan is periodically updated so that everyone sees the progress. After people become accustomed to using the Action Plan format, they discipline themselves. They do not want others to see that they are falling behind. This is a great time-saving and coordinating format. In Appendix C we present a sample strategic plan for Victory Christian Center to illustrate the development of strategies to accomplish a mission.

SUMMARY

A well-thought-out plan developed by everyone succeeds. How many times do you see churches and ministries trying to do everything at once? The word "strategic" in the title of this book implies thinking, praying, and seeking order. All this can happen if an Action Plan coordinates and supports the overall plan.

STRATEGY DEVELOPMENT WORKSHEET

This worksheet is provided to help you apply the concepts discussed in this chapter to your church or ministry.

<u>Answer These Questions First</u>

1. What are the distinctive competencies of your church/ministry? What do you do well?_____

_____

_____

_____

2. What market segment or segments should you select to match your church/ministry's skills and resources and constituents' needs in those segments?_____

_____

_____

_____

3. Do you have the skills/resources to pursue several segments or should you concentrate on one segment? Is that segment large enough to sustain your church/ministry and allow for growth?

_____

_____

_____

Now Develop Your Positioning Statement

1. Distinctive Competencies _____

_____

_____

2. Segments Sought _____

_____

_____

3. Services Offered _____

_____

_____

4. Promotion Orientation _____

_____

_____

5. Contribution Levels_____

_____

_____

6. Growth Orientation_____

_____

_____

Chapter 7

Evaluation and Control Procedures

Watch out that you do not lose what you have worked for, but
that you may be rewarded fully.

–2 John 1:8

The evaluation and control stage of the strategic planning process
can be compared to setting out on a journey with a road map. The
process includes identifying your destination (objective), determining the best route to your destination (strategy), and then departing
for your trip (implementation of your strategy). During the journey,
you look for highway signs (feedback) to tell you if you are on the
way to your objective. Signs along the way quickly reveal if you
have made a wrong turn, and you can alter your course to get back
on the right road. When you reach your destination, you decide on a
new route (strategy) to get you somewhere else.

Imagine what would happen if there were no road signs during
your trip to let you know if you were on the right road. It might be
too late to continue the trip by the time you realized you were
traveling in the wrong direction. Yet, many churches are involved in
a similar situation, failing to analyze results to determine if objectives are being accomplished.

Failure to establish procedures to appraise and control the strategic plan can lead to less than optimal performance. Many organizations fail to understand the importance of establishing procedures to
appraise and control the planning process. In this chapter we review
the need for evaluation and control, what is to be controlled, and
some control procedures. Evaluation and control should be a natural
follow-through in developing a plan (see Chapter 2). No plan
should be considered complete until controls are identified and the

procedures for recording and transmitting control information to administrators of the plan are established.

INTEGRATION OF PLANNING AND CONTROL

Planning and control should be integral processes. In fact, planning was defined as a process that included establishing a system for feedback of results. This feedback reflects the organization's performance in reaching its objectives through implementation of the strategic plan. The relationship between planning and control is depicted in Exhibit 7-1.

The strategic planning process results in a strategic plan. This plan is implemented (activities are performed in the manner described in the plan) and results are produced. These results include such things as attendance, contributions, and accompanying constituent attitudes, preferences, and behaviors. Information on these results and other key result areas is given to administrators, who compare the results with objectives to evaluate performance. In this performance evaluation they identify the areas where decisions must be made to adjust activities, people, or finances. Through this decision making the administrators control the plan by altering it to accomplish stated objectives, and a new cycle begins. The information flows are the key to a good control system.

The last stage of the strategic planning process, then, is to appraise the church and each of its entities to determine if all objectives have been met:

- Have the measurable objectives and goals been accomplished?
- How far did actual performance miss the mark? Did the attainment of the objectives and goals support the overall purpose?
- Has the environment changed enough to change the objectives and goals?
- Have additional weaknesses been revealed that will influence changing the objectives of the organization?
- Have additional strengths been added or your position improved sufficiently to influence the changing of your objectives?
- Has the ministry provided its members with organizational rewards, both extrinsic and intrinsic?

• Is there a feedback system to help members satisfy their high-level needs?

Timing of Information Flows

The strategic plan is supported by operational plans. If each of our operational plans is controlled properly, the strategic plans are more likely to be controlled. The administrator cannot afford to wait for the time period of a plan to pass before control information is available. The information must be available within a time frame which is long enough to allow results to accrue, but short enough to allow actions to align results with objectives. Although some types of organizations may find weekly or bimonthly results necessary, most organizations can adequately control operations with monthly or quarterly reports. Cumulative monthly or quarterly reports become annual reports, which in turn become the feedback needed to control the plan. Deciding what information is provided to which administrators in what time periods is the essence of a control system.

PERFORMANCE EVALUATION AND CONTROL

Performance should be evaluated in many areas to provide a complete analysis of what the results are and what caused them. Three key control areas are attendance, contributions, and constituents' attitudes. Objectives should have been established in all of these areas for the strategic plan.

Attendance Control

Attendance or audience control data are provided from an analysis of attendance for individual programs or services. Attendance can be evaluated on a program-by-program basis by developing a performance report as shown in Exhibit 7-2. When such a format is used, the attendance objectives stated in the plan are broken down on a quarterly basis and become the standard against which actual attendance results are compared. Number and percentage variations

EXHIBIT 7-1
Planning and Control Process

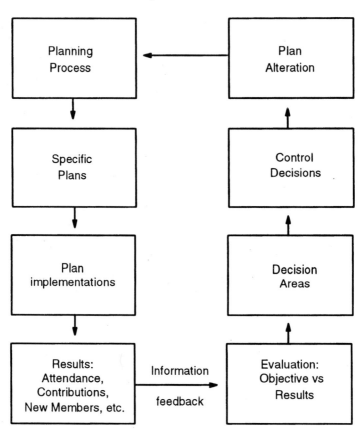

are calculated, because in some instances a small percentage can result in a large number variation.

A performance index can be calculated by dividing actual attendance by the attendance objective. Index numbers near 1.00 indicate that expected and actual performance are about equal. Numbers larger than 1.00 indicate above-expected performance, and numbers below 1.00 reveal below-expected performance. Index numbers are especially useful when a large number of programs are

		EXHIBIT 7-2			
		Attendance and Performance Report			
		Quarter 1 (By Program)			
Program	Attendance Objective	Actual Attendance	Variation	% Variation	Performance Index
A	1000.	900.	100.	−10.0	.90
B	950.	1020.	+ 70.	+ 7.4	1.07
C	1200.	920.	−280.	−23.0	.77
D	2000.	2030.	+ 30.	+ 1.5	1.02

involved, because they enable administrators to identify those programs which need immediate attention.

Contribution/Cost Controls

Several tools are available for establishing cost control procedures, including budgets, expense ratios, and activity costs analysis. Budgets are a common tool used by many organizations for both planning and control. The budget is often established by using historical percentages of various expenses as a percent of sales. Thus, once the total level of expected contributions is established, expense items can be budgeted as a percent of total sales. If zero-based budgeting is used, the objectives to be accomplished must be specified and the expenditures necessary to accomplish these objectives estimated. The estimates are the budgeted expenses for the time period.

Contributions are controlled by tracing gifts on a weekly or at least a monthly basis. While many organizations have an annual drive for pledges, others are continually seeking contributions from constituents. A prerequisite to controlling contributions is an annual projection of operating expenses. This projection, broken down on a quarterly or monthly basis, becomes the standard from which deviations are analyzed. For example, a church with a projected budget of 500,000 dollars for the next fiscal year would be expecting about 125,000 dollars per quarter, or 41,667 dollars per month.

If there were large variations related to certain times of the year, even the variations can be analyzed to determine the proportion of the budgeted amount given per month. If, historically, 20 percent of the budget was given during December, then 20 percent of next year's budget becomes the expected level of contributions to be used as the standard.

The same type of analysis used to control attendance (Exhibit 7-2) can be used to analyze data on contributions. This type of analysis should be performed on a timely basis to enable expansion or cutbacks of programs when contribution levels go above or below the expected amounts for the period.

Once the budget is established, expense variance analysis by line item or expenditure category is used to control costs. A typical procedure is to prepare monthly or quarterly budget reports showing the amount budgeted for the time period and the dollar and percentage variation from the budgeted amount, if any exists. Expenditure patterns which vary from the budgeted amounts are then analyzed to determine why the variations occurred.

Larger churches find revenue/expense centers to be a useful tool for control. For example, a church tape ministry generates revenues through the sale of tapes and incurs costs in recording, duplicating, and mailing out tapes; overhead; and labor costs. Tracking these revenues and expenses in a cost center would help control this ministry by letting the administrator know if it is breaking even or if it is generating excess revenues which could be used to expand the ministry or to lower the price of the tapes.

Constituent Feedback

The final area of performance evaluation is constituents, and involves analysis of awareness, knowledge, attitudes, and behaviors of members, participants, or supporters. Every organization should want its constituents to become aware of programs, services, or personnel; possess certain knowledge; and exhibit certain attitudes and behaviors. If these are specified in the objective statements, these objectives are the standards to which current constituent data are compared.

Data on constituents must be collected on a regular basis. There are many ways to collect data, but annual surveys are commonly used. Constituent data are especially valuable if collected over a long period of time, because awareness levels, satisfaction, attitudes, and behavior can be analyzed to reveal trends and areas for further investigation.

ESTABLISHING PROCEDURES

None of the performance evaluation data described are going to be available unless they are requested and funds are made available to finance them. Thus, data collecting and reporting procedures must be set up by the administrators who are going to use the control data in decision making.

The procedures will usually change over time as new types of analysis or reporting times are found to be better than others. The most important requirement is that the data meet the needs of administrators in taking corrective actions to control activities. With the expanded availability and use of computers by churches and ministries, much of the work can be computerized.

PERFORMANCE EVALUATION GUIDELINES

Keep these summary guidelines in mind when establishing an effective system for performance evaluation:

1. Performance evaluation must be self-evaluation;
2. Performance evaluation is for healthy, performing, growing individuals;
3. Evaluation is subjective;
4. "No evaluation" is not an option;
5. When an evaluation process is perceived as legitimate, fair, and working, people will tend to use it responsibly. When it is not, people will still do something, but they may not feel the burden of responsibility;
6. Performance evaluation is a formal process.

It is in the appraisal and control stage that churches and ministries really begin to see the benefits of the strategic concepts outlined in this book. When people at all levels know the progress being made toward fulfilling the overall plan, it creates a sense of pride, accomplishment, and excitement. Strategic planning will not work well without a review of performance.

SUMMARY

No planning process should be considered complete until appraisal and control procedures have been established. Performance evaluation is vital for control decisions. Information tells an administrator what has happened, and serves as the basis for any actions needed to control the activities of the organization toward predetermined objectives. Without such information, it is impossible to manage marketing activities with any sense of clarity about what is actually happening in the organization.

EVALUATION AND CONTROL WORKSHEET

This worksheet will aid you in applying the concepts discussed in this chapter to your church or ministry.

<u>Answer the Following Questions</u>

1. What kinds of information do you need to evaluate a program's or service's success?

_____

_____

_____

2. Who should receive and review this information?

_____

_____

_____

3. What time periods do you want to use to analyze the data? Weekly? Monthly?

_____

_____

_____

4. What record keeping system do you need to devise to make sure the information you want is recorded for the time periods you specified in question 3?

_____

_____

_____

NOW SET UP YOUR CONTROL PROCEDURES

1. Specify the areas to be controlled:

A. _____

B. _____

C. _____

D. _____

2. Specify the format of the data for each area. (Is it to be numbers by month by program? Do you want number and percentage variations?)

   A. _____

   B. _____

   C. _____

   D. _____

3. Specify how the data are to be collected, who is to collect and analyze the data, and who is to receive the results of the analysis:

   A. How will the data be collected? _____

   _____

   _____

   B. Who has responsibility to collect and analyze the data?

   _____

   _____

   _____

   C. Who is to receive which type of analysis?

Administrator/Pastor	Types of Analysis
1._____	1._____
2._____	2._____
3._____	3._____
4._____	4._____

References

Benjamin, D., J. Durkin, and D. Iverson. 1985. *The Master Builder.* Lake Tahoe: Christian Equippers International.

Boyce, L.F., ed. 1984. "Accounting for Churches." *Journal of Accountancy* (February), p. 96.

Buckingham, Jamie. 1982. "Having Visions–Dreaming Dreams." *Christian Leadership Letter.*

Burns, Cynthia F. 1992. *A Study of the Relationship Between the Use of Planning and Ministry Effectiveness in the Church.* Unpublished Thesis, Regent University.

"Cable Connections for Christ." 1985. *Charisma.* April, pp. 74-77.

"Defining the Mission." 1984. *Christian Leadership Letter* (June), pp. 1-2.

Drucker, Peter. 1954. *The Practice of Management.* New York: Harper.

Drucker, Peter. 1974. *Management: Tasks, Responsibilities, and Practices.* New York: Harper & Row.

Gray, Gary. 1983. "Managing for the Future." *Church Management* (August), pp. 10, 42.

Hale, Ashley. 1984. "Planning that Works." *Church Management* (September), p. 30.

Harvey, Phil, and J. Sander. 1987. "Charities Need A Bottom Line, Too." *Harvard Business Review* (January-February), vol. 65, pp. 14-22.

Lambert, N. M. 1975. *Managing Church Groups.* Dayton: Pflaum Publishing.

Lindgren, A. J. 1965. *Foundations for Purposeful Church Administration.* Nashville: Abingdon Press.

McConkey, D. D. 1978. *Goal Setting: A Guide to Achieving the Church's Mission.* Minneapolis: Augsburg Publishing House.

McDonough, Reginald M. 1975. *Leading Your Church in Long-Range Planning.* Nashville: Convention Press.

Migliore, R. Henry. 1988. *The Use of Strategic Planning for Churches and Ministries.* Tulsa: Harrison House.

Myers, F. Marvin, ed. 1983. "Trained Administrators Make a Difference." *Church Management* (March), p. 34.

Roberts, Evelyn. 1977. "How to Make 1977 the Most Exciting Year of Your Life." *Daily Blessing,* vol. 19, no. 1, pp. 10-11.

Schaller, L. E. 1965. *The Local Church Looks to the Future.* Nashville: Abingdon Press.

Shelly, M. 1985/86. "What's A Body To Do?" *Leadership* (Winter).

Thompson, Arthur A., Jr., and A. J. Strickland. 1986. *Strategy Formulation and Implementation,* 3rd edition. Plano, Texas: Business Publications, Inc.

Van Auken, Philip, and S. G. Johnson. 1984. *Church Administration* (May/June), p. 85.

Wesley, John. 1743. *The Nature, Design, and General Rules of the United Societies.*

APPENDIXES

Appendix A:
Biblical References
to the Planning Process

Exod. 9:16–But I have raised you up for this very purpose, that I might show you my power and that my name might be proclaimed in all the earth.

Deut. 1:22–Then all of you came to me and said, "Let us send men ahead to spy out the land for us and bring back a report about the route we are to take and the towns we will come to."

Josh. 22:3–For a long time now–to this very day–you have not deserted your brothers but have carried out the mission the LORD your God gave you.

1 Sam. 26:23–The LORD rewards every man for his righteousness and faithfulness.

Neh. 2:4–The king said to me, "What is it you want?" Then I prayed to the God of heaven . . .

Neh. 4:9–But we prayed to our God and posted a guard day and night to meet this threat.

Job 42:2–I know that you can do all things; no plan of yours can be thwarted.

Ps. 33:11–But the plans of the LORD stand firm forever, the purposes of his heart through all generations.

Ps. 37:4–Delight yourself in the LORD and he will give you the desires of your heart.

Ps. 105:4–Look to the LORD and his strength; seek his face always.

Prov. 11:14–For lack of guidance a nation falls, but many advisers make victory sure.

Prov. 13:13–He who scorns instruction will pay for it, but he who respects a command is rewarded.

Prov. 13:16–Every prudent man acts out of knowledge, but a fool exposes his folly.

Prov. 14:8–The wisdom of the prudent is to give thought to their ways, but the folly of fools is deception.

Prov. 14:15–A simple man believes anything, but a prudent man gives thought to his steps.

Prov. 14:22–Do not those who plot evil go astray? But those who plan what is good find love and faithfulness.

Prov. 15:22–Plans fail for lack of counsel, but with many advisers they succeed.

Prov. 16:2–All a man's ways seem innocent to him, but motives are weighed by the LORD.

Prov. 16:3–Commit to the LORD whatever you do, and your plans will succeed.

Prov. 16:9–In his heart a man plans his course, but the LORD determines his steps.

Prov. 16:20–Whoever gives heed to instruction prospers, and blessed is he who trusts in the LORD.

Prov. 16:32–Better a patient man than a warrior, a man who controls his temper than one who takes a city.

Prov. 17:24–A discerning man keeps wisdom in view, but a fool's eyes wander to the ends of the earth.

Prov. 18:15–The heart of the discerning acquires knowledge; the ears of the wise seek it out.

Prov. 19:8–He who gets wisdom loves his own soul; he who cherishes understanding prospers.

Prov. 19:20–Listen to advice and accept instruction, and in the end you will be wise.

Prov. 19:21–Many are the plans in a man's heart, but it is the LORD's purpose that prevails.

Prov. 20:18–Make plans by seeking advice; if you wage war, obtain guidance.

Prov. 21:5–The plans of the diligent lead to profit as surely as haste leads to poverty.

Prov. 22:3–A prudent man sees danger and takes refuge, but the simple keep going and suffer for it.

Prov. 24:3–By wisdom a house is built, and through understanding it is established . . .

Prov. 24:4–. . . through knowledge its rooms are filled with rare and beautiful treasures.

Prov. 24:5–A wise man has great power, and a man of knowledge increases strength . . .

Prov. 24:6–. . . for waging war you need guidance, and for victory many advisers.

Eccles. 7:25–So I turned my mind to understand, to investigate and to search out wisdom and the scheme of things and to understand the stupidity of wickedness and the madness of folly.

Eccles. 10:10–If the ax is dull and its edge unsharpened, more strength is needed but skill will bring success.

Isa. 14:24–The LORD Almighty has sworn, "Surely, as I have planned, so it will be, and as I have purposed, so it will stand."

Isa. 32:8–But the noble man makes noble plans, and by noble deeds he stands.

Isa. 40:29–He gives strength to the weary and increases the power of the weak.

Isa. 40:31–. . . but those who hope in the LORD will renew their strength. They will soar on wings like eagles; they will run and not grow weary, they will walk and not be faint.

Isa. 46:11–From the east I summon a bird of prey; from a far-off land, a man to fulfill my purpose. What I have said, that will I bring about; what I have planned, that will I do.

Isa. 48:15–I, even I, have spoken; yes, I have called him. I will bring him, and he will succeed in his mission.

Isa. 55:11–. . . so is my word that goes out from my mouth: It will not return to me empty, but will accomplish what I desire and achieve the purpose for which I sent it.

Jer. 29:11–"For I know the plans I have for you," declares the LORD, "plans to prosper you and not to harm you, plans to give you hope and a future."

Jer. 32:19–. . . great are your purposes and mighty are your deeds. Your eyes are open to all the ways of men; you reward everyone according to his conduct and as his deeds deserve.

*Matt. 6:33–*But seek first his kingdom and his righteousness, and all these things will be given to you as well.

*Luke 14:28–*Suppose one of you wants to build a tower. Will he not first sit down and estimate the cost to see if he has enough money to complete it?

*Acts 5:38–*Therefore, in the present case I advise you: Leave these men alone! Let them go! For if their purpose or activity is of human origin, it will fail.

*Rom. 8:28–*And we know that in all things God works for the good of those who love him, who have been called according to his purpose.

*1 Cor. 3:8–*The man who plants and the man who waters have one purpose, and each will be rewarded according to his own labor.

*1 Cor. 3:14–*If what he has built survives, he will receive his reward.

*1 Cor. 14:33–*For God is not a God of disorder but of peace. As in all the congregations of the saints . . .

*Gal. 3:3–*Are you so foolish? After beginning with the Spirit, are you now trying to attain your goal by human effort?

Eph. 5:16–. . . making the most of every opportunity, because the days are evil.

Phil. 2:2–. . . then make my joy complete by being like-minded, having the same love, being one in spirit and purpose.

Phil. 2:13–. . . for it is God who works in you to will and to act according to his good purpose.

Phil. 3:14–I press on toward the goal to win the prize for which God has called me heavenward in Christ Jesus.

Phil. 4:13–I can do everything through him who gives me strength.

Col. 2:2–My purpose is that they may be encouraged in heart and united in love, so that they may have the full riches of complete understanding, in order that they may know the mystery of God, namely, Christ . . .

Col. 3:23–Whatever you do, work at it with all your heart, as working for the Lord, not for men . . .

Col. 3:24–. . . since you know that you will receive an inheritance from the Lord as a reward. It is the Lord Christ you are serving.

Col. 4:5–Be wise in the way you act toward outsiders; make the most of every opportunity.

2 Thess. 1:11–With this in mind, we constantly pray for you, that our God may count you worthy of his calling, and that by his power he may fulfill every good purpose of yours and every act prompted by your faith.

2 Tim. 3:17–. . . so that the man of God may be thoroughly equipped for every good work.

Rev. 22:12–Behold, I am coming soon! My reward is with me, and I will give to everyone according to what he has done.

Appendix B:
Outline of a Strategic Plan

STRATEGIC PLANNING AND MANAGEMENT
WORKSHEET

I. Purpose

What is "reason for being," your "missions," why needed, customers served, needs met in marketplace, scope of the endeavor; nationwide, local, ethics, profit, or nonprofit.

_____

_____

_____

(Proverbs 29:18)

II. Environmental Analysis

A. _____

_____

B. _____

_____

C. _____

_____

D. _____

_____

(Proverbs 25:2)

III. Strengths and Weaknesses

    A. Human

    _____

    _____

    B. Facilities/equipment

    _____

    _____

    C. Patents/resources natural

    _____

    _____

    D. Financial

    _____

    _____

(Luke 12:48)

IV. Assumptions

    A. _____

    _____

    B. _____

    _____

    C. _____

    _____

        1. _____

        _____

2. _____

_____

3. _____

_____

V. Objectives and Goals

   A. Specific, time frame, measurable in key result areas.

_____

_____

(I Corinthians 14:40)

VI. Strategy–Two to three strategies for each objective.

   A. _____

_____

    1. _____

_____

    2. _____

_____

   B. _____

_____

    1. _____

_____

    2. _____

_____

_____

C. _____

_____

   1. _____

_____

   2. _____

_____

(Matthew 5:15)

VII. Operational Plans and Controls

A. _____

_____

B. _____

_____

(2 Timothy 2:15)

VIII. Reward/Performance Appraisal

A. _____

_____

B. _____

_____

(I Corinthians 3:8)

Appendix C:
Sample Strategic Plan
for Bellmar Church

STATEMENT OF PURPOSE

Bellmar Church is a non-profit church organization, consisting of a local body of believers with a vision to impact our metropolitan area and the world through the Holy Spirit's ministry of reconciliation to God, through Jesus Christ.

The purpose of Bellmar Church is to minister to the needs of people by

1. bringing people to salvation
2. ministering love, acceptance, forgiveness, healing, and deliverance
3. training, equipping, and preparing believers to do the work of the ministry

This purpose of service to people will be fulfilled through worship and praise, prayer, preaching and teaching, fellowship, and evangelism.

Worship and Praise

According to *Matthew 22:37*, the first and greatest commandment is to love God with all our heart, soul, and mind. Ministry to the Lord comes before ministry to people, and shows that Jesus is our "first love." God has called every believer to a life of praise. "This people have I formed for myself, they shall show forth my praise" (*Isaiah 43:21*).

Prayer

Prayer is a crucial element of the Christian life. When believers spend time in prayer, spiritual maturity, Godly direction, and miracles result. Bellmar's emphasis on prayer includes prayer during worship services, intercessory prayer groups, and daily morning prayer meetings, as well as frequently teaching and exhorting believers to pray (*Matthew 16:18-19*).

Preaching and Teaching

Believers are equipped and developed by the Word of God. Bellmar seeks to constantly nurture believers so that they can grow into full Christian maturity, and is committed to raising up strong spiritual, academic, and physical leaders through the preaching and teaching of God's Word (*Ephesians 4:11-12*).

Fellowship

The Scriptures liken the church to a living body, in which each member needs the other members in order to fulfill the purposes of the body. Likewise, each member of Bellmar needs the fellowship of others in order for the body to grow and develop. Bellmar is committed to providing an environment conducive to fellowship, and to meeting individual needs through small group fellowships (*1 Corinthians 12:12*).

Evangelism

Worship, prayer, fellowship, and teaching serve to prepare God's people for evangelism. Bellmar is committed to fulfilling the Great Commission to reach the unsaved with the message that God loves them, and sent His Son for them. Since the return of Jesus Christ is imminent, the fields are white unto harvest, the time is short, and God's people must work diligently to win the lost for Him (*Mark 16:15*).

ENVIRONMENTAL ANALYSIS

Economic Analysis

The second quarter report published by the Metro Economic Watch presents a broad view of the area's current economy. Competition between businesses has increased due to the sluggish economy. Though the economic conditions have improved only slightly, hiring is increasing in ten of the 11 areas studied (in all but mining). Energy is one of the state's assets in that it is inexpensive and plenteous. The other side of the energy coin, though, must be classified as a liability in that oil prices are continuing to decline. When considering the area's export products, the United States has a trade deficit. Many jobs have been lost recently through plant layoffs. Another economic concern is the state farm plight.

The national economic environment is growing, but sluggishly. Some of the federal funds budgeted have been shifted from military to social programs. Annual growth in defense spending will be trimmed to between 3 and 4 percent. The average hours worked figure is creeping upward. Productivity is slowly expanding. Businesses are being utilized at a high percentage of capacity but this is expected to decline slightly. Corporate cash flow and spending for plant and equipment are holding steady. The after-tax profits of non-financial firms will be down 10 percent for the remainder of this year. Corporations should be able to avoid a profit squeeze since labor costs are under control. Wages are climbing at about the same rate as productivity is growing. The pre-tax return on capital will decline to 7.4 percent in this fiscal year. Return on investment is almost as high as it has been in 17 years at 5.6 percent after-tax profitability. Capital intensity has increased faster than productivity, primarily due to increased global competition.

A broad overview of current global economic conditions reveals the following facts. Europe is resisting the fast pace of technological change, and is therefore lagging behind the more economically progressive countries such as Japan and the United States. China is moving into the world marketplace very slowly and cautiously. Trade with China has more long- than short-term potential. Slow growth and high unemployment will probably continue for several years. Japan is seeking to strengthen the yen against the dollar which will tend to reduce the U.S. trade deficit. Third-world debt appears to be less of a danger to lender countries because of long-term restructured schedules which assume a 5 to 6 percent economic growth rate in the Third World. Currently those living in Marxist countries make up 40 percent of the world's population. These nations, however, account for only 10 percent of world trade. Because of the inefficiencies of the socialist economic system, excessive military spending, and suppression of human rights (including forced labor), any hope for future improvement looks bleak. This is especially true for many war-torn countries such as Vietnam, Cambodia, Afghanistan, Ethiopia, and Nicaragua.

World oil prices should remain flat, so the cost of crude oil to refiners in the United States should remain relatively constant. While this is a benefit to American consumers, it has widespread negative implications for the local economy.

Demographic Analysis

Population

The total population of the county increased from 470,500 to 509,700. Most of the population growth occurred in the outlying neighborhoods, although the area just west of the river near the downtown area also recorded a substantial increase. Declines were recorded to the north and east of the downtown area. Much of the loss in these neighborhoods can be attributed to the displacement of housing units for urban development and expansion of the downtown highway network.

Population figures for the metro market, as of the end of year, are as follows:

	Totals	Rank
City population	374,100	74th in the nation
Suburban population	364,300	61st in the nation
Metropolitan statistical area population	738,400	64th in the nation
One person households	71,300	
Total households	281,000	

Housing

The number of housing units in the area increased substantially, with the largest growth in occupied housing units in the south and southeast suburbs. In the past years decline has been evident in the central city and areas to the north and northeast. This decline has resulted from the loss of residential units due to urban development, highway system improvements, and the expansion of the regional airport. Most recently, expansion has occurred between 1st and 2nd streets near the church.

Real Estate

In the past six months, the area real estate market has been moving slowly, and analysis confirms the presence of a buyer's market. The average listed price for a house was 102,000 dollars, while the average sale price was 97,000 dollars. Because of transition in many industries, a substantial number of families have had to move out of the area, and put their homes up for sale.

According to a recent newspaper article, brighter times are on the way. "All signs point toward a year of steady, if not spectacular, growth for the area economy," says real estate analyst Bill Smith. "In real estate, we've begun a modest recovery; it's slow, but it's beginning."

The city's Department of Civil Development's analysis predicts that

- real personal income should increase 1.2 percent, two times the rate for the previous year;
- total employment should rise 2 percent. At the same time, the unemployment rate should drop from 7.4 to 6.9 percent;
- total deposits at area banks should rise 6.2 percent to 4.92 billion dollars;
- retail sales should increase 3.8 percent;
- the value of construction contracts awarded should rise 8.9 percent to 1.2 billion dollars;
- there will be a modest increase in population and a net increase of approximately 4,800 jobs added in the area.

Comparative Analysis

As a congregation, Bellmar can be classified as a local church with a worldwide impact. The church's position, therefore, is largely a matter of comparison within the area.

Our city has long been known as a "city of churches," with one of the highest church density rates of any major city in the country. Approximately 700 congregations can be found in the metro area.

Two distinctly different groups of churches can be identified. The first group is comprised of those churches that serve residents in close proximity to Bellmar. Church growth planners indicate that approximately 80 percent of church attenders will not drive more than five miles to services. (Bellmar is an exception to this fact in that approximately 48 percent of the congregation lives more than five miles from the church.) A search of the *City Directory* and the *Yellow Pages* shows there are 53 churches within a 3.5 mile radius of our area. While these churches vary widely as to doctrine, style of worship, and denominational affiliation, all are vying for a share of the aggregate market within that geographical area.

The second group consists of large, charismatic churches that are perceived as offering similar worship opportunities, programs, and pastoral services. Six such churches have been identified: Farley Chapel, Christian Temple, Higher Life Fellowship, First Assembly of God, Avery Fellowship, and First Methodist Church.

Each of these churches was contacted by telephone to determine what programs or services it offers that are distinctive. This survey showed that these churches display a great deal of similarity in their programs and services. Some of the areas in which Bellmar appears to have enhanced programs are (1) Home Fellowship groups–two of the six churches have no such emphasis, which is a major factor in Bellmar's mission; (2) Christian schools–only two of the six have a Christian school. Neither of these schools include the senior high grades; (3) Street Outreach–only two of the six have a regular street witnessing program; (4) recreational programs–only three of the competitors have a gymnasium, and only two of those have regular recreational programs.

At the same time, Bellmar does not offer some programs that other churches feel are distinctive. First Methodist boasts three such programs: a feeding program; a large, well-respected counseling center; and a large, well-stocked, permanently staffed library. In addition, three of the six churches have extensive local television ministries.

Despite these minor differences in programs, the main comparative factor is one of style rather than substance. Each of these congregations has its own style of worship and fellowship. They all have dynamic, vibrant, strong-willed senior pastors, who, while sharing these similar traits, also have widely differing pastoral styles. In most cases, those who settle down at one or another of these congregations do so because they feel comfortable with the style of the church, rather than because of specific programs.

The main problem is that of commitment. Large churches find it difficult to develop consistent loyalty among attenders. There is a large group of Christians who frequent several of these large churches, sometimes even settling down at one or another for a short period of time. Without the commitment of these Christians, a potentially valuable resource is lost to these congregations. In addition, this group of migratory Christians often results in record-keeping difficulties for the church, including wide variations in attendance figures.

ASSUMPTIONS

No long-range plan will be successful if the assumptions on which it is based are not clearly stated. Thus, in the case of Bellmar, three major assumptions have been identified. From most important to least important, these are:

1. Joe Jones will continue to be the Senior Pastor;
2. The school board will continue to allow Bellmar to use the school for worship services and supporting ministries;
3. There will be no changes in local, state, or national laws that will adversely hinder the programs or ministry of Bellmar.

PROFILE OF CONGREGATION

As part of the information-seeking process for this plan, a lengthy survey was developed in conjunction with Bellmar's Long-

Range Planning Committee. The purpose of this survey was to obtain a profile of the congregation, and to determine the effectiveness of various programs. Program effectiveness will be explored in the "Strengths and Weaknesses" section of this plan, while the profile of the congregation is as follows:

- 53 percent are under age 35, while only 5 percent are 65 or older
- 52 percent of the families have only one or two members
- 48 percent have attended Bellmar one year or less, while 65 percent have attended two years or less
- 54 percent of members have been members for one year or less, 71 percent for two years or less
- 52 percent live within five miles of the church, 78 percent within ten miles
- 48 percent have lived at their current address for one year or less, 78 percent for five years or less
- 73 percent expect to reside in the area permanently
- 31 percent are singles, while another 8 percent are single parents
- 43 percent of female respondents work full time, and only 22 percent are homemakers; 7 percent are unemployed
- 60 percent of male respondents are employed full time, with another 17 percent being self-employed, and 10 percent unemployed (some of which are college students)
- only 9 percent did not finish high school, while 36 percent have obtained at least one college degree
- most college students are enrolled in the local community college
- 53 percent first heard of Bellmar through a friend, while only 10 percent first heard of Bellmar through some type of advertising
- 77 percent first attended Bellmar during a regular service, 9 percent during a crusade and 7 percent first came to hear a special speaker
- 91 percent of members and 78 percent of non-members have been baptized in water

- 95 percent of members and 83 percent of non-members have received the Baptism in the Holy Spirit
- There was a significant difference in the attendance habits of members and non-members in regard to Sunday morning, Sunday evening, and Sunday school attendance. The difference on Wednesdays was insignificant
- 46 percent of respondents never attend Sunday School, while 35 percent go an average of four times per month
- 33 percent never attend a Bible Fellowship group, while 47 percent go four times per month

STRENGTHS AND WEAKNESSES

Strengths

The major strength of Bellmar is its ability to meet people's needs. The diversity of the church, its staff, and its programs make it possible to meet a wide variety of needs. In addition, Bellmar has numerous strengths in particular areas.

Financial

1. Excellent record of giving, including gifts to missions
2. The increase in giving has been proportional to attendance growth
3. Well-defined and equitable employee compensation structure
4. Improvement in inventory turnover ratio from 104:1 to 107:1
5. Improvement in current ratio from 1.59:1 to 6.99:1
6. Improvement in acid test ratio from 1.37:1 to 6.86:1
7. Improvement in times interest earned ratio from 1.66:1 to 4.25:1
8. Decrease in debt ratio from 72 to 11.44 percent
9. Increase in fixed asset turnover from 1.0:1 to 12.67:1
10. Increase in total asset turnover from .93:1 to 2.53:1
11. Increase in surplus from 7.8 to 11.51 percent
12. Increase in return on assets from 7.32 to 29.13

Human

1. The charisma, vision, leadership, and delegation ability of the Senior Pastor
2. The pastor's wife is a strong co-paster, has good musical ability, and is loved by the congregation
3. Excellent leadership development process is made possible through Bible Fellowship groups
4. Capable administrative leadership
5. Strong outreach and evangelism leadership emphasis
6. Human resource expertise in areas of ministry to singles, men, women, children, teenagers, etc.
7. Expertise in finance and administration
8. Opportunity for everyone to get involved through home fellowship groups and extensive volunteer opportunities
9. Influence on college students in congregation yields vast expertise when student stays in the area and continues attending Bellmar
10. High rate of volunteer involvement

Spiritual

1. Missions emphasis provides spiritual strength:
   a. outreach ministries
   b. training programs
   c. financial support
2. Spiritual encouragement and training through Bible Fellowship groups
3. Emphasis on prayer (both early morning and intercessory groups)
4. Ability to demonstrate the love of God to everyone
5. Every member is contacted personally at least once per month
6. 80 percent of congregation feel spiritual needs are being met
7. 91 percent rate the Sunday morning service as "Very Good" or "Excellent"
8. 83 percent rate the worship portion of the services as "Very Good" or "Excellent"
9. Altar counseling is given high ratings by 79 percent
10. The annual crusade receives a 91 percent approval rating

Market Position

1. Bible Fellowship groups offer specialized ministries and opportunities for involvement
2. People feel welcome at Bellmar (93 percent agreed with the survey statement, "I feel welcome at Bellmar")
3. Special music is highly rated by 79 percent of survey respondents
4. Pastoral counseling is highly rated by 77 percent of survey respondents
5. The Children's Church for ages four and five is highly rated by 81 percent of survey respondents
6. The Nursery is highly rated by 82 percent of respondents
7. Excellent personal contact rate, as shown by the fact that over half of survey respondents first heard of Bellmar through a friend
8. Bellmar is effectively marketed through evangelism programs and street and tract ministry
9. Unique tape and bookstore ministry
10. Ability to minister to the entire family, including special programs such as Bellmar Christian School, Bellmar Bible Institute, and Bellmar World Ministries Training Center
11. Advantage of close ties to the local community college

Facilities

1. Access to a major auditorium
2. Excellent school and office facilities

Equipment

1. Excellent computer facilities
2. Modern videotaping and television equipment

Weaknesses

Organizational

1. Lack of effective planning system

2. Poor communication of tasks and responsibilities to employees
3. Lack of consistent goals, objectives, and strategies
4. Lack of affiliation with an organization or denomination leaves church in a potentially weak situation should a major conflict or staff disruption occur
5. Internal structures and procedures have not kept pace with numerical growth

Financial

1. Average collection period has increased 345 percent in the past two years
2. Surplus is highly volatile, and fluctuates much more widely than changes in attendance

Human

1. Lack of effective coordination of human resources
2. Lack of effective training for church employees
3. Lack of documented procedures in many areas
4. Above average rate of personnel turnover (partially due to transitory nature of workers who perceive Bellmar as a training center)
5. No employee has responsibility for marketing efforts

Spiritual

1. A substantial percentage of average attendance is due to transient or uncommitted persons
2. Low commitment from many college students who view Bellmar only as a convenient location to fulfill church attendance requirements
3. Less than 50 percent of average Sunday attendance is committed to a Bible Fellowship group, and 34 percent of the survey respondents gave the Bible Fellowship groups a low rating
4. Spiritual vitality of church largely dependent on personality of Senior Pastor

5. 35 percent of survey respondents give the Sunday School a low rating

Market Position

1. Many people perceive the large size of Bellmar to be a drawback
2. Single's ministry is not reaching the potential (100,000 singles live in the area). In addition, 45 percent of the survey respondents gave low ratings to the singles' ministry, and 42 percent gave a low rating to singles activities
3. The youth program may not be as strong as it should be. 40 percent of survey respondents gave low ratings to the youth services and activities
4. The adult recreation program is weak. 52 percent of respondents gave the program a low rating
5. Women's Ministries received a low rating from 40 percent of respondents
6. Men's Ministries received a low rating from 38 percent of respondents, and Men's Breakfasts received a low rating from 36 percent of respondents
7. Children's Church (ages six to 12) received a low rating from 33 percent of respondents
8. The Bellmar Bible Institute night program received a low rating from 30 percent of respondents
9. The financial counseling program received a low rating from 30 percent of respondents

OBJECTIVES, STRATEGIES, AND PLANS

Both the ministry of the church to its members, and the outreach of the church to the community, come about through the various programs of the church. Just as a profit-oriented company is able to continue in existence by meeting needs with its product, the church achieves its purposes through the various services and programs that it provides.

The programs of the church have been identified as to their stage in the product life cycle. The fact that most of Bellmar's programs fall into the introduction or growth stage bodes well for the long-range ability of the church to meet the needs of the congregation and of the community.

Attendance

There is no such thing as an industry comparable to Bellmar, nor are comparative figures for churches readily available. Much of the financial analysis, therefore, consists of educated opinions and projections.

The two most important figures to consider when planning revenue for a large church are the average Sunday morning attendance, and the average revenue per attender per year. In this plan, all percentages for involvement or attendance are based on average Sunday morning attendance.

Objective

Four attendance projections have been produced. The pessimistic forecast is based on a 10 percent average growth rate, the most likely forecast is based on a 20 percent growth rate, the optimistic forecast is based on a 30 percent growth rate, and a "faith" forecast is based on a 35.8 percent growth rate, which is the rate that would be required in order for the church to reach its publicly stated goal of 20,000 by the end of the century.

Average Total Sunday Morning Attendance

Type of Forecast	Year 1	Year 2	Year 3	Year 4	Year 5
Pessimistic (10%)	4756	5232	5755	6330	6963
Most Likely (20%)	5189	6226	7472	8966	10760
Optimistic (30%)	5621	7308	9500	12350	16055
"Faith" projection (35.8%)	5872	7974	10829	14706	20000

The objective is to achieve the most likely attendance for each year between 1994 and 1998.

Strategy

Attendance is a variable dependent on program strategies, therefore, individual strategies are presented under the program section.

To attempt to calculate objectives for key financial ratios at this point in time would not be relevant to the major financial objectives of the organization.

Productivity

Objectives

1. To maintain a ratio of one full-time equivalent staff member per 100 average Sunday morning attendance. This figure does not include staff for the Christian School. Just as many businesses have a target labor cost percentage, church management experts state that a church should have one pastoral staff member for every 200 of average attendance, along with support staff, for a total ratio of 1 to 100.
2. To reach the following percentages of laity involvement by these dates:

	Year 1	Year 2	Year 3	Year 4	Year 5
Percentage of lay people actively involved in ministry	27%	29%	31%	33%	35%

Strategies

1. Compare yearly average attendance figures with number of full-time equivalent employees, and adjust to within target percentages
2. Encourage lay involvement by:
   a. establishing a computerized file which categorizes members by various skills, and actively recruit their aid as needed for special projects
   b. emphasizing current lay training opportunities offered by Bellmar Mission Training Center
   c. making facilities and specific staff members available for use by volunteers
   d. providing recognition for volunteers by sending thank-you notes, publishing names in church mailings, etc.

Operating Plans

1. Director of Finance will make yearly calculation of employee/attendance ratio, and have responsibility for keeping staff levels within a reasonable variance
2. Monthly reminders to directors to recognize all significant volunteer efforts and skill contributions

Personnel

Objectives

1. Establish quarterly Staff Development Seminars
2. Send staff members to observe the operation of another church throughout the year, and have them report their findings to their department
3. Send each director once each year to a national conference related to their area of responsibility, in order to facilitate a state-of-the-art operation
4. Involve directors in ten hours per month of training, along with a quarterly retreat
5. Establish a performance appraisal system by the end of the year. Annual salary reviews should be correlated with the performance appraisal system

Strategies

1. Invite key speakers to present workshops on relevant staff development topics
2. Seek out churches that are strong in areas of perceived weaknesses, and allow staff members to profit from these organizations' expertise
3. Director's training will focus on increasing ability of each director to accomplish the goals of his/her unit and of the church. Various methods may include videotaped seminars, teaching tapes, and speakers
4. See Performance Appraisal section for strategy details relating to reward system and salary review policies

Operating Plan

1. Administrative Team will assume responsibilities for personnel development. Specific assignments include responsibility for developing quarterly workshops starting at the beginning of the year, and structuring weekly director's meetings to include relevant training materials

Spiritual

Objectives

1. By mid-year, implement an accurate record-keeping system for the number of salvations
2. Achieve the following objectives for salvations through these areas:

Outreach	Year 1	Year 2	Year 3	Year 4	Year 5
Altar/Sanctuary	1500	1800	2160	2592	3732
Street Witnessing	800	880	968	1065	1288
Special Missions	500	600	700	800	900
Relational	1000	1200	1440	1728	2488
TOTALS	3800	4480	5268	6185	8408

3. Have 60 percent of average attendance involved in Bible Fellowship Groups each week
4. Objective for number of Bible Fellowship Groups (calculated by multiplying the average Sunday attendance by 60 percent, then dividing by an average of 12.5 people per group):

Outreach	Year 1	Year 2	Year 3	Year 4	Year 5
Bible Fellowship Groups	250	300	360	430	515

5. Have a weekly training session for Bible Fellowship group leaders, and a meeting with the Pastor

6. Establish a yearly retreat, with the Pastor, for all Bible Fellowship group leaders
7. Implement policy of tuition waiver for Bible Fellowship group leaders to attend Bellmar Bible Institute. Policy should be in place by mid-year

Strategies

1. Strategy for record-keeping of salvations:
   a. commitment card to be filled out for each conversion, either by the worker or by the new Christian
   b. yearly all-church survey should include a question concerning the number of salvations each member has produced
2. Strategy for reaching salvation goals:
   a. salvation emphasis in each church service, with regular altar calls
   b. recruitment of volunteers for street witnessing
   c. promote at least two special missions projects each year
   d. training in relational witnessing to be offered at least twice each year
3. Strategies for Bible Fellowship group goals:
   a. Bellmar currently practices the strategy of geographical segmentation of their target market by zip code. This strategy is in agreement with McKinsey's principle of territorial "classification of activities"
   b. the Pastor should continually emphasize Bible Fellowship groups from pulpit
   c. train Bible Fellowship group leaders to challenge their groups to accomplish spiritual, relational, and evangelistic functions
   d. encourage training of Bible Fellowship group leaders through a yearly retreat with the Pastor
   e. offer incentives for additional training through tuition waiver at Bellmar Bible Institute

Operating Plans

1. Development of a plan for tallying salvations by the end of the first quarter

2. Inclusion of salvation tally in yearly church survey
3. Evangelism Coordinator will develop a six-week relational evangelism seminar by April. Seminars will be offered several times each year
4. Date for first yearly retreat for Bible Fellowship group leaders will be set by February
5. By January, the Director of Pastoral Care and the Assistant Director for BBI will set up tuition waiver program for Bible Fellowship group leaders

Organizational

Objectives

1. Begin implementing Management By Objectives at all levels of the organization by January
2. Begin bi-weekly meetings for each director with his/her immediate subordinates by January

Strategies

1. Implementation of MBO:
   a. after church long-range plan has been approved, MBO should then be gradually extended downward through the organization
   b. each person in organization should write out personal job objectives, and negotiate with immediate superior
2. Directors should be required to meet with subordinates every two weeks, so that the vision, goals, and current needs of the organization can be effectively communicated, and the needs of the subordinates can be dealt with

Operating Plans

1. By April, the Long-Range Plan Committee will have developed and implemented procedures for extending MBO throughout the organization
2. Each supervisor will have responsibility for implementing MBO in their area by June

Programs

Programs are an essential part of a church's ministry and outreach, particularly in a large church. Programs are often the drawing card by which a family becomes involved in, and later committed to, the church. As part of this plan, an extensive survey was distributed to the congregation. One major purpose of the survey was to determine which programs the congregation feels are strong, and which are in need of improvement. The survey results indicate that most of the program areas of the church are relatively strong. The following objectives seek to strengthen areas that are perceived to be weak, and to develop some new areas of ministry.

Objectives

1. By March, make singles' activities available two nights/week
2. By March, develop a plan for regular adult recreational activities
3. Decrease dissatisfaction with the youth program, as measured by the annual survey, by 10 percent in the next year
4. Decrease dissatisfaction with Women's and Men's Ministries, as measured by the annual survey, by 10 percent in the next year
5. Develop comprehensive plan for the Financial Counseling program by July 1

Strategies

1. Singles Ministry holds great potential for Bellmar, since there are approximately 100,000 singles in the area
   a. it is necessary to have singles' activities available several times each week in order to accommodate the flexible lifestyle of singles, and integrate them into the congregation
   b. promote annual Single's Explosion
   c. encourage single's ministry to develop their own outreaches to minister to the community, and to reach other singles
2. Bellmar currently has excellent recreational facilities. The Athletic Director should be commissioned to develop a weekly adult recreational program

3. Department heads of the Youth, Men's Ministries, and Women's Ministries departments should use a personal interview method to determine the reasons for a high level of dissatisfaction with their departments
4. Because finances are an important part of modern life, the church should recruit laypeople with expertise in this area, and set up periodic seminars on this topic, as well as offer individual financial consulting to families in the church

Operating Plans

1. By June, Singles' Pastor will develop comprehensive plan for reaching the unsaved singles of the area
2. By March, the Athletic Director will develop plan for weekly adult recreational program
3. By March, the department heads of the Youth, Men's Ministries, and Women's Ministries will submit results of their investigation into causes of dissatisfaction with their departments, and negotiate a plan of action with their superiors
4. Director of Finance will be given responsibility for developing the Financial Counseling program. Will submit plan for this area by July 1, with first special seminar scheduled for September

Promotional

Objectives

1. Reach one-third of the metropolitan area with advertising by end of the year
2. Increase local and national recognition of church by 20 percent by the end of the year
3. Develop comprehensive marketing plan by end of the year

Strategies

1. Enlist the congregation to participate in door-to-door evangelism, covering the entire target area, using a planning map

2. Continue distribution of fliers and tracts
3. Billboard advertising to increase local recognition
4. Make concerted effort to receive good publicity through secular media
5. Continue involvement in TV shows, which leads to national recognition for the church

Operating Plan

1. By the end of the year, the church should hire a specific individual as the Director of Marketing, with responsibility to develop a comprehensive marketing plan by the end of the year
2. Evangelism Director will continue responsibility for distribution of fliers and tracts, and develop a plan for door-to-door coverage of the city by the end of the year

APPRAISAL OF OPERATIONS

An appraisal of Bellmar for the past year reveals that a large part of its continued success is the Senior Pastor's ability to communicate the church's vision to its members. Emphasis was placed on the members' involvement in the five major areas of the church's purpose statement: (1) worship, (2) prayer, (3) fellowship, (4) teaching, and (5) evangelism. There were positive results in each of these five areas, yet the increase in laity involvement did not meet the desired level.

The budgeting system was another area that needed improvement. The budget did not provide the adequate, detailed information necessary to operate a large, nonprofit organization.

The area that most exemplifies the spiritual strength of Bellmar is the Bible Fellowship groups. There was tremendous growth in this area last year. A large part of this growth can be attributed to the specific goal-setting for the number of groups. Nevertheless, survey results indicate that the small group concept has not been fully accepted by the congregation. Since the Bible Fellowship groups are integral to accomplishing Bellmar's goals and objectives, this lack of acceptance is a cause for both concern and action.

Overall, Bellmar is in a period of tremendous growth and opportunities. The church is young and vibrant, with much potential. The addition of a long-range planning process should do much to help Bellmar obtain its potential.

PERFORMANCE APPRAISAL

Currently, Bellmar has already taken two major steps on the road toward a fair and productive performance appraisal system. First, it is using an extensive job rating classification scheme. Each position is assigned to one of 50 different categories, which determines the salary range for that position. Second, each employee of Bellmar currently receives an annual performance review. Salary increases are based on job performance. This yearly review is an opportunity for the supervisor and employee to get together and evaluate performance.

Nevertheless, additional steps must be taken in order to have an effective performance appraisal system. The first step in this process is to have each staff member write out individual job objectives in order of priority. This list will then be negotiated with the immediate supervisor. The individual job objectives must be consistent with the goals and objectives of the ministry.

Once an agreement has been reached, both parties will sign and date the agreement. Mile markers should be established to monitor progress between the quarterly performance appraisals. The supervisor will use the previous agreement to evaluate the worker's performance and to determine if objectives were met.

Rewards are based on the conclusions from the quarterly evaluations. The best rewards are intrinsic rewards, which come about as a natural result of the management by objectives process, for instance, workers gain a high level of satisfaction from achieving the goals they have set for themselves. Other rewards, such as plaques or written recognition, are appropriate for outstanding performance.

Extrinsic rewards are more difficult to implement under an MBO system. Nevertheless, extrinsic rewards can play an important role in the performance appraisal reward process. Bellmar's current salary administration program utilizes extrinsic rewards in its yearly salary review. With the implementation of MBO into the entire organization, the reward system should be adjusted to consider the quarterly performance appraisals in the yearly salary evaluation. Other extrinsic rewards, such as paid vacations, should also be a part of the reward system.

One possible extrinsic reward that is extremely applicable to a church organization is to establish an "Employee of the Year Award," with a trip to the Holy Land as a prize. This attractive, yet spiritually based reward could be a major incentive to employee productivity.

Appendix D:
Planning and Management Systems Audit

I. Purpose

    A. Is it written? _____

    B. Does it define boundaries within which your church/ministry operates? _____

    _____

    C. Does it define the need(s) that your church/ministry is attempting to meet?_____

    _____

    D. Does it define the market that your church/ministry is reaching?_____

    _____

    E. Do you intend to have local, regional, national, or international scope? _____

    _____

    F. Has there been input from others?_____

    _____

    _____

G. Does it include the word "service," or a word with similar meaning?_____

_____

_____

II. Environmental Analysis
  A. Have you listed several international/national trends that affect your church/ministry?_____

_____

_____

  B. Have you listed several local trends that affect your church/ministry?_____

_____

_____

  C. Have you identified trends unique to your church/ministry?
    1. Membership? _____

_____

    2. Active and inactive members? _____

_____

    3. Average attendance at various services?_____

_____

    4. How many baptized, deaths, new members, transfers, and so forth?_____

_____

    5. Sunday School or Bible Study attendance?_____

_____

  D. Have you listed several of your most important "competitors"?

1. Which are growing?_____

_____

2. Which are declining?_____

_____

3. What are the successful ones doing?_____

_____

III. Strengths and Weaknesses for each area:
   A. People _____

   _____

   B. Spiritual _____

   _____

   C. Financial _____

   _____

   D. Facilities _____

   _____

   E. Equipment _____

   _____

IV. Functional Analysis
   A. Financial Analysis
      1. What is your current financial situation?_____

      _____

      a. Do you have regular financial statements prepared?

      _____

      _____

2. What tools would be beneficial in analysis? _____

_____

_____

   a. Do you have pro forma statements for profit centers such as a bookstore, day care, etc.? _____

   _____

   b. Do you have a cash budget? _____

   _____

   c. Do you have a capital budget? _____

   _____

   d. Has a ratio analysis been prepared?_____

   _____

   e. Do you understand the time value of money?_____

   _____

   f. Do you understand and use break-even analysis? ____

   _____

3. Have you analyzed current financial policies?_____

_____

   a. Do you have cash policies? _____

   _____

   b. How are accounts receivable analyzed? _____

   _____

   c. How are accounts payable analyzed? _____

   _____

   d. Do you control inventory levels? _____

   _____

e. Do you have a debt retirement plan? _____

_____

4. What is a synopsis of your current financial situation?

_____

_____

B. Accounting Analysis
  1. Analysis of current accounting policies
    a. Depreciation procedures? _____

    _____

    b. Tax considerations? _____

    _____

    c. Decentralized/centralized operations? _____

    _____

    d. Responsibility accounting? _____

    _____

  2. Tools beneficial in analysis
    a. Do you have budgets (short- and long-range) estab-
       lished? _____

    _____

    b. Do you perform variance analysis? _____

    _____

    c. What costing methods are used? _____

    _____

    d. Do you do contribution margin analysis? _____

    _____

3. What is your synopsis of the current accounting situation? _____

_____

4. Are there adequate controls, especially of cash at Sunday services? _____

_____

C. Market Analysis

1. Have you established marketing policies? What you will and won't do? _____

_____

a. Have you identified you consumers? _____

_____

b. Who are your competitors? _____

_____

c. Product: type of ministry, type of demand, market position: _____

_____

d. Distribution and location of facilities? _____

_____

e. Pricing and contributions? _____

_____

f. What promotion (advertising, and selling) activities are you using? _____

_____

2. What is your synopsis of current marketing situation?

_____

_____

D. Management Analysis

1. Plan – Do you have a planning system? How does it work? _____

   _____

2. Organize – Is organization of resources correct? _____

   _____

3. Is control centralized or decentralized? _____

   _____

4. What staff needs do you have? _____

   _____

5. Are controls in evidence? What are they? _____

   _____

6. Is there a motivation problem? _____

   _____

7. Is strategy defined? What is strategy now? _____

   _____

8. What is your synopsis of the current management situation? _____

   _____

9. How efficient are operations? _____

   _____

V. Other areas of analysis

A. Computer Systems

1. Do you need a computer system? _____

   _____

2. In what areas will it be used? _____

   _____

    a. Membership lists _____

    b. Mailings _____

    c. Financial systems _____

    d. Information systems _____

    e. Inventory control _____

    f. Networking _____

B. Legal Analysis – Do you know the laws affecting churches/ ministry? _____

_____

C. Insurance, buildings, automobile liability, and so forth?

_____

_____

VI. Objectives

A. Are they in key result areas? _____

_____

B. Are the objectives specific, measurable, and for a set time frame? _____

_____

C. Are there long- and short-term objectives? _____

_____

VII. Strategies – Do you have several strategies for each key result area? List them. _____

_____

_____

_____

_____

Appendix E:
Sample Church/Ministry Questionnaires

ADULT SUNDAY SCHOOL SURVEY

FIRST, PLEASE ANSWER THESE QUESTIONS THAT PERTAIN TO THE CLASS YOU BELONG TO.

1. What class are you a member of?
   __ Saints and Sinners   __ Fellowship Class
   __ Joynor Class   __ Seekers Class
   __ Beacon Class   __ Asbury Class
   __ Circle Class   __ New Covenant
   __ Builders Class

2. What is the approximate size of the class?
   __ 10 or less   __ 11-15   __ 16-20   __ 21-25   __ 26 +

3. The class would be most effective if it were:
   __ larger   __ the same size   __ smaller

4. How often do you attend your Sunday School class?
   __ 1 time a mo.   __ 2 times a mo.   __ 3 times a mo.   __ every
                                                               week

---

NOTE: These are sample questionnaires shown only to demonstrate the types of questions which can be asked in various forms. They are intended to be used as tools to gain insight into members'/viewers' perceptions of services they are exposed to.

5. In a typical month, how many times would your class meet other than in church?
__ none __ 1 time __ 2 times __ 3 times __ 4 times __ 5 times

6. The length of the terms for officers should:
__ be increased   __ stay the same   __ be decreased

7. I feel comfortable (accepted) in the class.
(agree)   1   2   3   4   5   6   7   (disagree)

8. The class is very organized.
(agree)   1   2   3   4   5   6   7   (disagree)

9. Too much time is spent on "class business."
(agree)   1   2   3   4   5   6   7   (disagree)

THE NEXT QUESTIONS EVALUATE ALL THE CLASSES WHICH ARE OFFERED INCLUDING THEIR TEACHERS.

PLEASE EVALUATE EACH CLASS YOU HAVE ATTENDED SINCE LAST JUNE.

SUBJECT: "God's Plan for the Family"

10. I thought the class topic was interesting.
(agree)   1   2   3   4   5   6   7   (disagree)

11. The material was difficult to understand.
(agree)   1   2   3   4   5   6   7   (disagree)

12. More time should have been spent in lecture.
(agree)   1   2   3   4   5   6   7   (disagree)

13. More time should have been spent in discussion.
(agree)   1   2   3   4   5   6   7   (disagree)

14. The teacher's apparent knowledge in subject taught was good.
   (agree)   1   2   3   4   5   6   7   (disagree)

15. The teacher was always prepared for class.
   (agree)   1   2   3   4   5   6   7   (disagree)

16. The teacher was interested and enthusiastic in the subject.
   (agree)   1   2   3   4   5   6   7   (disagree)

17. The teacher was able to convey meaning of subject matter well.
   (agree)   1   2   3   4   5   6   7   (disagree)

18. The teacher was open to new ideas.
   (agree)   1   2   3   4   5   6   7   (disagree)

19. The teacher was a good leader.
   (agree)   1   2   3   4   5   6   7   (disagree)

20. My general evaluation of the teacher is excellent.
   (agree)   1   2   3   4   5   6   7   (disagree)

21. This teachers rates very high in comparison to other teachers.
   (agree)   1   2   3   4   5   6   7   (disagree)

22. My general evaluation of this class is excellent.
   (agree)   1   2   3   4   5   6   7   (disagree)

23. This course rates very high in comparison to others.
   (agree)   1   2   3   4   5   6   7   (disagree)

24. I would recommend this teacher to my friends.
   (agree)   1   2   3   4   5   6   7   (disagree)

25. I would recommend this class to my friends.
   (agree)   1   2   3   4   5   6   7   (disagree)

26. I would recomnmend this teacher for this course.
    (agree)   1   2   3   4   5   6   7   (disagree)

27. It is important that this class is offered.
    (agree)   1   2   3   4   5   6   7   (disagree)

28. The Bible could have been used more in this class.
    (agree)   1   2   3   4   5   6   7   (disagree)

29. I benefited intellectually from this class.
    (agree)   1   2   3   4   5   6   7   (disagree)

30. I benefited spiritually from this class.
    (agree)   1   2   3   4   5   6   7   (disagree)

31. What aspect of the life of the church do you personally find most helpful?
    __ Sunday Worship Service   __ Social fellowship
    __ Sermons   __ None
    __ Music programs   __ Other (specify)
    _____

32. What do you consider to be the major strengths of the adult Sunday School program?

33. What do you consider to be the major weakness of the adult Sunday School program?

34. What recommendations would you suggest for improving the adult Sunday School program?

35. What would you like to see taught next year?

    In order for us to make use of the materials you have completed, we need a little information concerning you. This will be confidential and is for purposes of statistical tabulation only. Check appropriate categories or write in the necessary answers.

36. What is your age? _____   Male __   Female __

37. What is the highest level of education you have attained?
Grade School __   College Degree __   Other _____
High School __   Graduate Degree __

38. Present Employment Status:
__ Employed   __ Housewife
__ Self-employed   __ Student
__ Unemployed   __ Retired

39. If you are employed or self-employed, what kind of work do you do (or position held)?

_____

_____

40. What is you home zip code? _____

41. How long have you been attending this church?
Less than 1 yr. __   1-10 yrs. __   11-20 yrs. __
21-30 yrs. __   31 + yrs. __

42. How often do you attend the morning worship service?

Never attended	1-10 times a yr.	At least 1/mo.	At least 2/mo.	At least 3/mo.	Almost always
_____	____	__	__	__	_____

43. Which service do you usually attend?
9:50 __   10:50 __

44. How often do you attend both the morning service and Sunday School?
Always__ Most of the time__ Some of the time__ Never __

45. What is your marital status?
Single __   Married __   Divorced __   Widowed __

46. Please classify yourself as one of these three types of Christians:

    __ Traditional: Stresses the importance of RITUAL concerning Christian practice as governed by the HISTORICAL and defined AUTHORITY of the Church.

    __ Evangelical: Stresses the importance of PREACHING, emphasizing SALVATION through faith in the death of Jesus Christ through personal conversion and SHARING this faith with others.

    __ Charismatic: Stresses the importance of SPIRITUAL RENEWAL of power (as of healing) given a Christian by the HOLY SPIRIT for the good of the Church.

47. Which five of the following would you choose as the marks of a mature Christian? Place (1) to the left of the most important, (2) to the left of the next most important and so on to (5).

Do not mark more than five and do not mark any equally. If you have items of your own not covered in this list, add them at the bottom and give them a number among your five choices.

Do not number more than five including any you write in. We regard all of these as important marks of a Christian. You are to choose among these really important things those which are the five most important to you.

    __ 1. Belonging to the Church

    __ 2. Having a correct belief about God

    __ 3. Loving and serving his fellow man

    __ 4. Having a correct belief about the Bible

___ 5. Engaging in personal prayer

___ 6. Obeying his ecclesiastical superiors

___ 7. Having a conscious experience of fellowship with God

___ 8. Giving to the church

___ 9. Having a correct belief about Jesus

___ 10. Teaching his children the right things to believe

___ 11. Living joyfully from day to day

___ 12. Receiving the sacraments regularly

___ 13. Having a right belief about life after death

___ 14. Remaining confident amid distress and difficulty

___ 15. Attending church services regularly

TV SURVEY

Hello, I'm _____, and I'm from _____, an opinion research company in _____. We are conducting an opinion survey for a TV ministry in order to assist them in being even more responsive to the needs of the viewing public. I would like to ask you a few questions about your opinions toward religious organizations and their importance in your life. Your answers will be kept confidential and will be used only to determine general trends among the attitudes of those folks we survey. There are no right or wrong answers, so your frank and candid opinions are very important. If at any time you don't understand a question, stop me and I'll gladly repeat the question.

----

1. Which, if any, of the following religious TV programs have you watched in the last 30 days? (READ LIST IN GRID BELOW UNDER "TV MINISTRIES" AND CIRCLE APPROPRIATE NUMBER UNDER "Q1").

TV MINISTRIES	Q1	Q2	Q3	Q4
Billy Graham	1	1	1	1
Oral Roberts	2	2	2	2
Robert Schuller (Hour of Power)	3	3	3	3
Jerry Falwell (Old Time Gospel Hour)	4	4	4	4
Bob Tilton	5	5	5	5
Richard DeHahn (Day of Discovery)	6	6	6	6
Pat Robertson (700 Club)	7	7	7	7
None	0	0	0	0

2. Of these same TV ministries, which have you written a letter to in the last 30 days? (RE-READ LIST IN GRID AND CIRCLE APPROPRIATE NUMBER UNDER "Q2)

3. Of these TV ministries mentioned, which program meets your needs better than any other? (RE-READ LIST IF NEC- ESSARY AND CIRCLE APPROPRIATE NUMBER UNDER "Q3")

4. Of these television ministries, which, if any, have you contrib- uted money to in the last year? (RE-READ LIST IF NEC- ESSARY AND CIRCLE APPROPRIATE NUMBER UNDER "Q4")

5. How often do you watch religious TV programming? (READ CHOICES, CIRCLE APPROPRIATE NUMBER)

   1. Several times a week   4. Several times a year

   2. Once a week   5. Never

   3. Once a month

6. Now, thinking back to the last 30 days, how many Sundays did you watch a televised religious program? (WAIT FOR RESPONSE BEFORE READING CHOICES, THEN CIRCLE APPROPRIATE NUMBER)

1. 1 time   4. 4 times

2. 2 times   5. 0 times

3. 3 times

7. As I read the following statements regarding religious television programs, tell me whether you, strongly agree, somewhat agree, somewhat disagree, or strongly disagree. (READ CHOICES, 1, STRONGLY AGREE, 2, SOMEWHAT AGREE, 3, SOMEWHAT DISAGREE, 4, STRONGLY DISAGREE. DON'T READ DON'T KNOW!!)

	Strongly Agree	Somewhat Agree	Somewhat Disagree	Strongly Disagree	DON'T KNOW
a. The donations are always spent for worthy projects.	1	2	3	4	(5)
b. Religious TV programs ask for money too often.	1	2	3	4	(5)
c. Television ministers answer your letters in a personal manner.	1	2	3	4	(5)
d. These programs have too many write-in gimmicks.	1	2	3	4	(5)

e. TV ministers really
   help you with your
   spiritual needs.   1   2   3   4   (5)

f. Some programs are
   becoming too
   "Hollywood" or
   polished.   1   2   3   4   (5)

g. The sermons and
   teachings could be
   improved.   1   2   3   4   (5)

h. Their emphasis has
   shifted too much from
   the spiritual to
   entertainment.   1   2   3   4   (5)

i. Fund raising by TV
   ministries through
   telethons is a good
   idea.   1   2   3   4   (5)

j. TV ministries send
   out too much mail.   1   2   3   4   (5)

k. Giving money to
   religious causes is
   more important than
   giving to any other
   cause.   1   2   3   4   (5)

l. TV ministers do
   not use donations
   for personal gain.   1   2   3   4   (5)

8. What could TV ministries do to better meet your needs?

_____

_____

9. During the past six months what percent of your total income did you contribute to religious TV ministries? (READ CHOICES AND CIRCLE)

1. Less than 1 %
2. 1 to 4%
3. 5 to 9%
4. 10% or more

5. None
6. REFUSED
7. DON'T KNOW

10. Please complete this statement: I would give more money to TV ministries if:

_____

_____

11. How many Sundays, in the past 30 days, did you attend a church service at your local church? (WAIT FOR RESPONSE BEFORE READING CHOICES AND CIRCLE APPROPRIATE NUMBER)

1. 1 time
2. 2 times
3. 3 times

4. 4 times
5. 0 times
6. DON'T KNOW

12. During the past six months what percent of your total income did you contribute to the church of your choice? (READ CHOICES)

1. Less than 1%
2. 1 to 4%
3. 5 to 9%

4. 10% or more
5. None
6. REFUSED

7. DON'T KNOW

13. If you were to give money to a charitable organization, how would you rank these in order of importance, i.e., 1 = most important, 2 = second most important, etc. (WRITE IN 1 THRU 6) (ROTATE) (READ CHOICES)

Religious TV ____

United Way ____

Health Organizations ____

Churches ____

Overseas Mission ____

Don't Know ____

14. Which of the following best describes your employment status? (CIRCLE APPROPRIATE NUMBER)

    1. Full time   5. Homemaker

    2. Part time   6. Unemployed, currently
                                   between jobs

    3. Retired   7. Other
    4. Student   8. REFUSED

15. Are you: 1. Married (READ CHOICES)
               2. Widowed
               3. Separated
               4. Remarried
               5. Divorced
               6. Single
               7. REFUSED

16. Which of the following age categories do you fall within? (READ CHOICES)

    1. 18 to 34   4. 65 or older
    2. 35 to 49   5. REFUSED
    3. 50 to 64

17. Which of the following best describes your church preference? (READ CHOICES)

    1. Roman Catholic   5. Lutheran
    2. Jewish   6. Interdenominational
    3. Baptist   7. Other (SPECIFY)

    _____

    4. Methodist   8. REFUSED

18. Which of the following income categories best describes your total household income before taxes? (CIRCLE APPROPRIATE NUMBER AND STATE THAT THEIR NAMES ARE NOT KEPT AND THAT THE INFORMATION IS GROUPED)

1. 5,000 or less

2. 5,001 to 10,000

3. 10,001 to 15,000

4. 15,001 to 25,000

5. Over 25,000

6. REFUSED

7. DON'T KNOW

19. Have you ever made a personal commitment to Jesus Christ?

1. Yes (GO TO 20)

2. No (THANK YOU AND TERMINATE)

3. Don't Know (THANK YOU AND TERMINATE)

20. Is that commitment still important today?

1. Yes (GO TO 21)

2. No (THANK YOU AND TERMINATE)

3. Don't Know (THANK YOU AND TERMINATE)

21. Do you feel that your commitment to Jesus Christ was a turning point in your life?

1. Yes

2. No

3. Don't Know

Name _____ City _____
      (only for validation)

Phone No. _____ Interviewer's Initials _____

Index